SUPER SIMPLE SCIENCE EXPERIMENTS
FOR CURIOUS KIDS

100 Awesome Activities
Using Supplies You Already Own

SE 0 6 '22

SUPER SIMPLE
SCIENCE
EXPERIMENTS
FOR CURIOUS KIDS

ANDREA SCALZO YI
Bestselling author of *100 Easy STEAM Activities*

BARRINGTON AREA LIBRARY
505 N. NORTHWEST HWY.
BARRINGTON, ILLINOIS 60010

PAGE STREET
PUBLISHING CO.

Copyright © 2022 Andrea Scalzo Yi

First published in 2022 by
Page Street Publishing Co.
27 Congress Street, Suite 1511
Salem, MA 01970
www.pagestreetpublishing.com

All rights reserved. No part of this book may be reproduced or used, in any form or by any means, electronic or mechanical, without prior permission in writing from the publisher.
Distributed by Macmillan, sales in Canada by The Canadian Manda Group.

26 25 24 23 22   1 2 3 4 5

ISBN-13: 978-1-64567-571-6
ISBN-10: 1645675718

Library of Congress Control Number: 2021951124

Cover and book design by Meg Baskis for Page Street Publishing Co.
Photography by Lucy Baber

Printed and bound in the United States

 Page Street Publishing protects our planet by donating to nonprofits like The Trustees, which focuses on local land conservation.

DEDICATION

For Tony and our never-ending sources of inspiration:
Nate, Dylan, Oliver and Alexander.

Contents

Introduction ... 11

Chapter 1
Liquids — 13

Toothpick Star ... 14
Underwater Volcano ... 17
Upside-Down Water Cup ... 18
Perfect Circle ... 20
Bendy Straw ... 21
Three-Layer Bubbles ... 23
Invisible Ink ... 24
Don't Spill the Water ... 25
Drinkable Density Experiment ... 26
Red Cabbage Experiment ... 28
Floating Paper Clip ... 30
Spin the Bowl ... 31
Magic Strainer ... 33
Floating Ping Pong Ball ... 34
Tornado in a Bottle ... 37
Oil and Ice Density ... 38
Swimming Fish ... 39
Drops on a Penny ... 40
Floating Orange ... 43
Ocean in a Jar ... 44

Chapter 2
Solids — 47

Growing Crystals ... 48
How Strong Is an Eggshell? ... 50
Tear the Paper ... 51
Straw in a Potato ... 53
One-Sided Paper: Möbius Strip ... 54
Spinning Eggs ... 56
Make a Copper-Plated Nail ... 57
Banana Secret Message ... 59
Spinning Forks ... 60
Balancing Can ... 63
Magic Twirling Paper ... 64
Sprouts in a Bag ... 67
Pencils Through a Baggie ... 68
Standing on Eggs ... 71
Inertia Checkers ... 72
Separating Salt and Pepper ... 73
Floating Heart ... 74
Wall Marble Run ... 77
Ice Tunnels ... 78
Ice Cream in a Bag ... 80
Straw Wrapper Worms ... 81
Blue Coins ... 83
Balancing Forks ... 84
Coin in the Bottle ... 86
Notepad Friction ... 87
Balloon Skewers ... 89
Jumping Shapes ... 90
Spin a Penny in a Balloon ... 92

Spinning Pencil	93
Turn Milk into Plastic	95
Floating Drawings	96
Clean the Pennies	97
Fluffy Slime	98
Oobleck	101
Rubber Egg	102
Craft Stick Explosion	104
Floating Ring	107
Egg Drop	108
Potato Skewer Balance	111
Whip Off the Napkin	112
Melting Ice with Pressure	113

CHAPTER 3
GASES 115

Smoking Bubbles	116
Dry Paper Experiment	119
Fill the Balloon	120
Lifting with Air	122
Diving Ketchup Packet	123
Blow Paper in a Bottle	125
Don't Open the Bottle	126
Exploding Baggie	128
DIY Fire Extinguisher	129
Soda Volcano	131
Can Crusher	132
Lemon Volcano	135
Aluminum Foil Boat	136
Dissolving Seashells	137
Rising Water Candle Experiment	138

CHAPTER 4
LIGHT, COLOR & SOUND 141

String Art	142
Oil and Water Art	145
Egg Art	146
Wet and Dry Painting	147
Magic Milk	148
Coffee Filter Chromatography	151
Water Shapes	152
Fizzy Art	155
Fireworks in a Jar	156
Mixing Colors	159
Make a Sunset	161
DIY Rainbow	162
Playdough Color Mixing	163
Candy Rainbow	165
Hot/Cold Watercolor Mixing	166
Upside-Down Spoon Experiment	168
Disappearing Coin	169
Reverse the Image	170
Water Rainbow	172
Drawing a Perfect Circle	173
Ringing Spoon	174
Sun Prints	175
Pop a Balloon with a Sun Ray	176
Sound You Can See	177
Acknowledgments	179
About the Author	181
Index	183

Introduction

There's nothing my kids love more than doing experiments. I am constantly getting the request to set up an experiment for them, and it was the main reason I wrote this book. It's not always easy to come up with an experiment on the spot, and looking online can seem overwhelming with all the options.

Why is experimenting important? When you experiment, you ask questions, tinker, explore, make predictions and draw conclusions. All these skills are important for you to nurture and develop in order to become the great thinkers, inventors and leaders of tomorrow. Experimenting keeps your curiosity growing, and being a curious child is an important step in becoming an innovative, creative problem-solver.

This book is meant to be your go-to resource. With it, you have 100 simple experiments at your fingertips that you can easily do at school or at home, with items you already have. The experiments all demonstrate scientific principles and are simply explained. This keeps the learning at a high level and will give a basic idea of some core principles such as density, static electricity, surface tension and center of gravity, allowing you to learn and understand our world in new ways.

To my fellow parents, I like to let my kids look through the book and pick which experiment they want to do. This helps build excitement as we're setting it up and makes them feel like a part of the process. Younger kids will need more guidance, but older kids (ages 10+) will be able to set up and execute many on their own or with little help.

I hope you enjoy using this book to engage with your kids in simple, fun and educational ways. Some of my favorite moments with my kids have been when I've seen the lightbulb of learning go off while doing a delightful experiment. It's learning in action and there's nothing quite like it!

Chapter 1

LIQUIDS

Bringing science into your home with fun, simple experiments is a great way to spark curiosity in kids, introduce them to scientific concepts and spend quality time together engaging in educational activities! The experiments that follow are all SUPER easy to set up and most of them can be done with objects you already have at home. Are you ready? Let's go!

There are three states of matter that exist in the world: solids, liquids and gases. In this chapter, we'll explore liquids, which are defined as having a definite volume, but not a definite shape. They take the shape of the container they are placed in, and there are so many exciting ways to experiment with them!

Toothpick Star

Simplicity Level:

Here's a science experiment that's sure to amaze your friends and parents! You'll be taking five broken toothpicks and turning them into a star with just a few drops of water and the power of capillary action!

Materials

- 5 wooden toothpicks
- Shallow tray
- Dropper or pipette
- Water

Directions

Carefully break the toothpicks in half without breaking them all the way into two pieces. The pieces should still be attached and forming a V shape. Arrange them with their broken centers in the middle together on the shallow tray. Fill the dropper with water and slowly add some drops of water to the middle where all the broken toothpicks meet. Watch as the toothpicks try to straighten and form a star!

The Hows and Whys

The toothpicks are made of dried wood, and when you broke them in half, you stretched the wood fibers. When the fibers get wet, they absorb the water through capillary action, causing them to swell and try to straighten themselves out. Capillaries are the tiny tubes inside plants and trees that allow them to carry water to the entire plant. This causes the toothpicks to move and create the star formation.

Variations

Make new shapes with the broken toothpicks before adding water. Also, change the temperature of the water to see if it affects how quickly the star forms.

Underwater Volcano

SIMPLICITY LEVEL:

Volcanos are so amazing to watch! In this density experiment, you can make your own underwater volcano using hot and cold water and some food coloring!

Materials

- 2 clear glass or plastic containers, 1 large and 1 small enough to sit inside the large one
- Cold tap water
- Hot tap water
- 1 small rock
- Liquid food coloring
- Stick or chopstick

Directions

Fill the larger container three-quarters full of the cold tap water. Fill the smaller container with hot tap water. Place the small rock in the bottom of the small container to weigh it down. Add a few drops of food coloring to the small container and mix with the stick. (You can make your volcano any color you want, but mixing red and yellow will give you orange-like lava!) Gently place the small container into the large container and let it sink to the bottom. Watch the orange "lava" flow out from the small container into the large container. Notice how the orange "lava" stays at the top of the large container and doesn't sink to the bottom.

The Hows and Whys

Hot water or "lava" from the small container rises to the top of the large container because the molecules in the hot water move faster and therefore make it expand and become less dense.

Variations

Use water of the same temperature and see what happens. Also, make your cold water yellow and your hot water red and watch them mix when added.

Upside-Down Water Cup

SIMPLICITY LEVEL:

In this fun experiment, you're going to use a single piece of paper to hold a full glass of water upside down while keeping all the water from falling out! Sounds like magic, right? Well, it's actually due to the forces of pressure inside and outside the drinking glass.

MATERIALS
- 1 small clear drinking glass
- Water
- Index card or any stiff piece of paper just large enough to cover the opening of the glass

DIRECTIONS
You'll want to do this activity over the sink to prevent any spills. Fill the glass up to the very top with water. Make sure it's filled all the way to the brim. Place the index card on top of the glass so that it fully covers the opening. Keep your hand on top of the index card and flip the glass upside down. Remove your hand from the card and notice how the water stays in the glass!

THE HOWS AND WHYS
This water remains in the glass because the air pressure outside the glass is greater than the water pressure inside the glass. This means the forces pushing on the index card from the outside of the cup are stronger than those forces pushing on the index card from the inside of the cup, and therefore the card stays in place and holds the water in the cup.

VARIATION
Use different types and sizes of paper. What happens if you use a paper towel or a piece of paper much larger than the opening of the glass? Does it still work? Why or why not?

Perfect Circle

Simplicity Level:

Here's a simple way to use surface tension to create a perfect circle with a piece of thread.

Materials
- Glass baking dish
- Water
- 1 (12" [30-cm]) piece of thread
- Dish soap

Directions

Fill the glass dish halfway with water. Tie the thread ends in a knot so it makes a circle. Place the thread on the surface of the water in the dish. Notice how it forms an uneven circle. Place 1 drop of dish soap inside the thread circle. Amazingly, the thread immediately forms a perfect circle!

The Hows and Whys

The drop of dish soap placed in the thread's circle reduced the surface tension of the water inside the circle. This caused the water outside the circle that had a higher surface tension to pull the thread outward, which formed the thread into a perfect circle.

Variations

Make circles of different sizes. Be sure to wash the baking dish well between uses as residual soap in the dish can affect how well the experiment works. Also, use two thread loops. Does it work for both of them?

Bendy Straw

Simplicity Level:

Here's a fun trick you can do with your friends. Tell them you're going to bend a straw without even touching it!

Materials
- 1 clear drinking glass
- Water
- Straw

Directions
Fill the glass three-quarters full of water. Place the straw in the glass so that some of the straw is in the water and some is sticking out of the water. Examine the straw from the top down, looking into the glass. Everything looks normal, right? Now look at the straw from the side of the glass. At the point where the straw hits the water, it appears to be bent or broken! Finally, remove the straw from the water and it magically appears straight again.

The Hows and Whys
We see objects in the world because rays of light travel to our eyes and create an image. Light rays travel more slowly through water and glass, so the portion of the straw that appears in the water reaches our eyes later than the part of the straw out of the water. This is called refraction, and it refers to how the light bends as it travels through different substances. This causes the straw to appear bent or broken.

Variation
Test the straw in other liquids such as clear soda, corn syrup or rubbing alcohol.

Three-Layer Bubbles

SIMPLICITY LEVEL:

Blowing bubbles is a fun activity, but blowing a bubble inside a bubble inside a bubble is even more fun!

The Hows and Whys

Bubbles are made up of air wrapped in three layers that are soap, water and soap. These three layers work together to keep the bubble together, but if the water layer evaporates, then the bubble can't keep the surface tension and it pops! When you keep the counter surface wet, it allows the three outer layers of the bubble to stay intact and not pop. This is also why you can touch the bubbles with a wet finger. When you touch a bubble with a dry finger or object, it causes that water layer to evaporate and breaks the seal of the bubble, causing it to pop!

Materials
- Water
- Straw
- Bubble solution

Directions

Get the surface of a counter wet with water. Dip your straw far into the bubble solution to coat it. Gently blow into the straw to make a bubble near the wet spot on the counter. The bubble will start to form over the spot in a semicircle and sit on the counter without popping. Remove the straw and dip it in the bubble solution again. Insert the straw into the bubble and blow another bubble inside the first one. Be sure to keep the second bubble smaller than the first or it will pop the first one. Remove the straw from both bubbles. Dip the straw in the bubble solution one final time and insert it through both bubbles. Blow a third bubble inside the second one. Remove the straw and you have a bubble in a bubble in a bubble! Notice how the first bubble gets bigger each time you add new bubbles inside it. Touch your three-layer bubble with a finger coated in bubble solution. You can put your finger inside the bubble! Now touch your bubble with a dry finger. It pops!

Variations

See how many layers of bubbles you can blow inside each other. To make round bubbles, turn a plastic cup upside down, dip it in bubble mix and use it as a bubble stand. Add some food coloring to your bubble mix to make colorful bubbles!

Invisible Ink

Simplicity Level:

In this experiment, you'll be able to write secret, invisible messages to your friends that they will only be able to read when they heat up the paper!

Materials
- 1 lemon
- Small bowl
- Water
- Cotton swab
- White paper
- Lamp

Directions

Squeeze the juice of the lemon into the small bowl. Add a splash of water, and use the cotton swab to mix in the water. Then use the cotton swab to write a message on the white paper. The lemon juice will dry clear and your message will be invisible. To make the ink visible, hold the paper up to the warm lightbulb of the lamp and watch the message appear on the paper!

The Hows and Whys

Lemon juice contains carbon compounds that oxidize and turn brown when heated. The compounds are colorless when dissolved in water, but they break down when heated and produce carbon, which is brown or black. That's what makes your message appear on the paper!

Variation

Test other liquids such as milk, honey (watered down), orange juice or vinegar and see if they work in the same way.

Don't Spill the Water

SIMPLICITY LEVEL:

Do you think water will spill out of a bucket if it's upside down? Well, not if we harness the power of centripetal force!

The Hows and Whys

The water stays in the bucket due to centripetal force. Centripetal force is the force that acts on an object to keep it moving in a circular motion. In this case, it keeps the water moving in a circular motion, and it's stronger than the force of gravity, which is pulling the water to the ground. Therefore, the water stays in the bucket and keeps moving around the circle. This is the same force that keeps you in a roller coaster when it goes upside down and our planets rotating around the sun!

Materials

- Small bucket with a handle
- Water

Directions

You'll want to do this experiment outside as you'll need lots of room. Fill a small bucket (like you use at the beach in the summer) halfway full of water. Grab the bucket by the handle and with a quick motion, swing your arm in a full circle starting from your arm being down by your side and moving so it goes above your head and back down to your side again. The bucket should be in an upside-down position when your arm is above your head. What happened to the water in the bucket when it was upside down? Did it spill? No, it stayed in the bucket!

Variation

If you want to get wet, spin the bucket more slowly and see at what point the water will fall from the bucket.

Drinkable Density Experiment

Simplicity Level:

Here's a fun and yummy experiment to demonstrate how liquids with different densities don't mix, and in the end, you will even get to taste your delicious creation!

The Hows and Whys

The various juices stay separate in the glass because their sugar levels give them different densities. Higher sugar levels in a liquid make the liquid denser and therefore heavier. As less dense liquids are added, they stay sitting on top because they are lighter.

Variation

Use other drinks you have around your house to make more delicious density drinks. All you need to do is find liquids with various sugar levels. Try things such as coffee, water, soda and other juices.

Materials

- 3 juices with various sugar contents and colors (for example: white grape juice with 40 g of sugar, mango juice with 25 g of sugar and cranberry juice with 9 g of sugar)
- 4 clear drinking glasses
- Dropper or pipette

Directions

Pour ½ cup (120 ml) of each juice into separate glasses. Use the dropper to move some of the juice with the highest sugar content into the empty glass until it is one-quarter full. Next, use the dropper to move the juice with a medium sugar level into the same glass until it is half full. Place the dropper at the edge of the glass when releasing the liquid into the glass to help minimize mixing. Finally, use the dropper to add the lowest sugar content juice to the glass until it is three-quarters full. You will see how all the layers stay separate in the glass due to their various sugar contents. Now all that's left to do is drink your three-layer juice creation! If your first sip is too sour, it's because the cranberry juice is sitting at the top. You may want to mix all your juices together for a sweeter creation!

Red Cabbage Experiment

Simplicity Level:

Did you know that cabbage juice can be used as an indicator to test if a liquid is an acid or a base? In this fun experiment, we'll use cabbage juice to do just that!

The Hows and Whys

Cabbage juice is considered a pH indicator, which means it tells us if something is an acid or a base. It contains a chemical substance called anthocyanin. Acidic substances contain hydronium ions, and when cabbage juice encounters hydronium ions, it turns red, indicating an acid is present. Substances that are bases contain hydroxide ions, and when cabbage juice encounters a base, it turns blue or green.

Materials

- 1 red cabbage leaf
- Scissors
- Blender (for grown-ups to use)
- 1 cup (240 ml) water
- Strainer
- 1 clear drinking glass
- 5 small clear drinking glasses or test tubes
- 1 tsp baking soda
- 1 tsp sugar
- 1 tsp white vinegar
- 1 tsp lemon juice
- Tablespoon
- Dropper or pipette

Directions

To make the cabbage juice, cut up the cabbage leaf into small pieces with the scissors. Place in the blender along with the water and blend until it's liquified. Pour the mixture through the strainer into the glass to separate the juice from the pulp. Discard the pulp and keep the cabbage juice in the glass. Fill each of the 5 small glasses three-quarters full of water, and then add 1 teaspoon of the following to the glasses:

- glass 1: baking soda
- glass 2: sugar
- glass 3: nothing
- glass 4: white vinegar
- glass 5: lemon juice.

Use the dropper to add 1 tablespoon (15 ml) of cabbage juice to each of the 5 glasses and see what happens. If the solution turns blue or green, it is a base. If it turns red, it is an acid.

VARIATIONS

Make your own pH testing strips by adding cabbage juice to a coffee filter, letting it dry and then cutting it into small strips. Dip the strips into various liquids to test the pH levels. If the strip turns red, the liquid is acidic. If it turns blue or green, it is basic. Test different liquids around the house such as laundry detergent, orange juice, soda, etc.

Floating Paper Clip

SIMPLICITY LEVEL:

Does a paper clip float or sink in water? The answer is more complicated than you think . . . it's both! In this experiment, we'll discover why a paper clip can appear to both float *and* sink in water.

The Hows and Whys

Even though the paper clip appeared to be floating, it was actually just sitting on top of the water due to surface tension. Water molecules like to stick together, particularly on the surface, and because these molecules attract and stick together, the surface can support light objects such as a paper clip. Soap causes those water molecules to separate, so when you add soap to the water, the surface tension vanishes and the paper clip sinks. This is also why soap helps get dirty dishes clean!

Materials

- 1 clear drinking glass
- Water
- 1 paper clip
- Dish soap

Directions

Fill the glass 90 percent full of water. Gently place the paper clip on the surface of the water. Notice that the paper clip seems to float on top of the water. Now, remove the paper clip, and this time, place it just below the surface of the water. What happens? It sinks! How can it both float *and* sink in water? Remove the paper clip and place it once again on top of the water so it floats. Add 1 to 2 drops of dish soap to the water, making sure the soap is away from the paper clip. What happens to the paper clip? It sinks right as the soap hits the water!

Tip: If you're having trouble getting your paper clip to float, unfold one end of a second paper clip and use it as a tray to lower the paper clip into the water.

Variations

Find other steel objects around the house to do this experiment with, such as a straight pin. Also, see how many paper clips you can get to float on the water or use a straw to blow the paper clips around on the surface of the water. You can also try different types of liquids such as juice or milk and see if you get the same outcomes.

Spin the Bowl

SIMPLICITY LEVEL:

In this experiment, you'll use the power of centrifugal force to spin a bowl using just your finger and not touching the bowl!

MATERIALS
- Large bowl
- Water
- Small bowl

Directions
Fill the large bowl one-third full of water. Fill the small bowl one-third full of water and place it in the large bowl. The small bowl should float. Use your finger to swirl the water in the small bowl around in a circle without touching the edge of the small bowl. Notice the small bowl starts spinning. Spin your finger a little faster and watch the bowl pick up speed. Observe that when you spin the water fast, the water in the small bowl moves up the edges of the bowl until it's almost dry at the bottom of the bowl. When you stop spinning the water, it returns from the edges of the bowl.

The Hows and Whys
Because the small bowl is sitting in liquid, there is very little friction to stop it from spinning, so it spins very easily. The water in the small bowl moved up the side of the bowl when it was spinning fast due to centrifugal force. The water was trying to escape the bowl by moving to the outer edge of the circle as it spun faster and faster.

Variation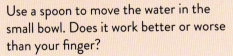
Use a spoon to move the water in the small bowl. Does it work better or worse than your finger?

MAGIC STRAINER

SIMPLICITY LEVEL:

In this experiment, you'll use the power of surface tension to keep water inside a water bottle covered only with mesh!

MATERIALS

- 1 empty clear bottle with a small neck (a glass soda bottle works great)
- 1 (4 x 4" [10 x 10-cm]) plastic mesh square, such as the kind fruit comes in (see photo)
- Rubber band
- Water
- Toothpick

DIRECTIONS

Cover the bottle with the plastic mesh square and secure it in place with the rubber band. Hold the bottle under a faucet and fill it with water. Place your hand over the mesh and flip the bottle upside down. Slowly remove your hand and notice that the water stays in the bottle! If the water comes out, you may need to make your mesh size smaller or double up the mesh to create smaller openings. While the bottle is still upside down, insert the toothpick through the mesh and into the bottle. Does any water leak out? Finally, slowly tilt the bottle to the side and keep tilting it until the water starts to pour out.

THE HOWS AND WHYS

The water stayed in the bottle when you removed your hand because of surface tension. Water molecules try to stick together due to a force called cohesion. The water molecules form a thin membrane between each of the openings of the plastic mesh, and this barrier keeps the water from falling through. Even when you inserted the toothpick, the surface tension stayed intact, and you probably only saw a small drop of water fall out of the bottle to make room for the toothpick. Once you start to tip the bottle, air comes in and breaks the surface tension, causing water to pour out the mesh.

VARIATIONS

Use different sizes of screens to see how large the holes can be to still make the experiment work. If you have a metal mesh strainer, use that instead of plastic mesh. Also, experiment with different bottles and opening sizes.

Floating Ping Pong Ball

Simplicity Level:

In this activity, your challenge is to get a ping pong ball to float in the center of a glass of water without touching it. Sounds easy enough, right? You may be surprised!

Materials
- 2 clear drinking glasses
- Water
- Tray or baking sheet
- 1 ping pong ball
- Dropper or pipette

Directions
Fill the glasses almost full of water and place them on the tray. Place the ping pong ball in the center of the water in one of the glasses. Does it stay in the center or move to the side? Try to get it to move to the center without touching it. You will notice it always moves to the edge. Fill the dropper with water from the other glass. Add that water slowly to the glass with the ping pong ball until the water forms a dome above the rim of the glass. What happens to the ping pong ball at this point? It floats to the center!

The Hows and Whys
Water doming at the brim of the glass is due to surface tension and the water molecules sticking together. When the water starts to dome, the ball floats to the highest point, which is the center of the glass!

Variation
Use other floating objects you have around the house, such as a cork.

Tornado in a Bottle

Simplicity Level:

Tornadoes occur outdoors when warm, humid air meets cold, dry air. While you can't create a real tornado, in this fun experiment you are going to make one appear in a jar of water and learn about centripetal force!

Materials

- 1 clear glass bottle with a lid that seals tightly
- Water
- Dish soap
- 1 tsp vinegar
- Glitter (optional)

Directions

Fill the bottle three-quarters full of water. Add a small squirt of dish soap, the vinegar and some glitter (if using). Seal the bottle so that no water leaks out. Shake the bottle in a circular motion and watch the tornado form.

The Hows and Whys

As you spin the bottle in a circular motion, a vortex is created in the middle as the water swirls around it. This is due to centripetal force, which is a force that keeps the water moving in a curved path that's directed toward the center of the bottle.

Variations

Add food coloring to your water to make a colorful tornado! You can also throw in some small beads or other objects and watch them swirl in the tornado.

Oil and Ice Density

Simplicity Level:

You probably already know that oil and water don't mix, but what happens when you add ice to the equation? Do the ice cubes float or sink in the oil? Let's experiment and find out!

Materials

- Water
- Ice cube tray
- Liquid food coloring
- 1 clear drinking glass
- Vegetable oil

Directions

Add water to the ice cube tray, and then add a drop of food coloring (pick your favorite color) to make the ice cubes a fun color. Put the ice tray in the freezer and wait until the cubes are frozen. Fill the glass one-quarter full of water, and then fill it the rest of the way with the vegetable oil. Drop 1 ice cube into the glass. If the ice cube has any air in it (which most do), it will float in the oil. If it sinks to the bottom of the oil, it means there is no air trapped in it. Try again with a different ice cube. What happens as the ice starts to melt? You will see a drop of colored water form at the bottom of the ice cube and then break away from the ice cube and fall through the oil to the water at the bottom of the glass.

The Hows and Whys

As the ice cube starts to melt, a drop of water starts forming at the bottom of the cube. Once it gets too heavy, it breaks off and forms a sphere of water that falls through the oil. You probably notice the drop first sat at the bottom of the oil for a bit and then eventually burst and trickled into the water at the bottom of the glass.

Variations

Add some salt to the top of the ice cube. Does this speed up the melting process? Warm up the oil a bit before starting this experiment. How does that affect the melting of the ice cube?

Swimming Fish

SIMPLICITY LEVEL:

In this experiment, you'll use the power of surface tension to make paper fish swim across a plate of water using only dish soap.

The Hows and Whys

Water molecules stick together and create surface tension. When soap hits water, it breaks the surface tension, so when you added a drop of soap near the fish's tail, it causes the surface tension to fall. This pushes the fish forward as the soap tries to disperse in the water. Once the soap is evenly dispersed throughout the water, the fish will stop moving.

Variations

Make other shapes with paper and get these objects to move in the water. Also, use a larger tray or pan and have multiple fish race across the tray.

Materials

- Water
- Shallow plate
- Scissors
- Construction paper
- Dish soap

Directions

Add water to the plate until it is half full. Use the scissors to cut out a fish shape in the construction paper, and make sure its tail has a bit of a triangle shape at the end. Lay the fish on the water so it floats. Add 1 drop of dish soap to the middle of the tail section of the fish. Watch the fish swim forward.

Drops on a Penny

Simplicity Level:

How many drops of water can a penny hold? Is it 5, 10, 20 or more? You might be surprised by the answer. In this experiment, you'll explore how many drops of water a penny can hold and learn about surface tension along the way!

The Hows and Whys

The penny with plain water held many more drops than the penny with soapy water because of surface tension. Water molecules stick together and create surface tension, which is what causes the surface of the water to bulge up a bit on the penny. Dish soap lowers the surface tension of the water and prevents that bulge from forming on the penny. Therefore, the penny with the dish soap mixture held less water than the penny with plain water.

Materials

- 2 pennies
- Tray or baking sheet
- 2 drinking glasses or cups
- Water
- Dropper or pipette
- Dish soap

Directions

Place the pennies on the tray. Fill both glasses halfway with water. Use the dropper to collect water from one of the glasses. Drip the water onto one of the pennies, one drop at a time, to see how many drops you can add before the water spills over. You will notice a dome of water start to form over the penny before it finally flattens and overflows. Add a squirt of dish soap to the water in the second cup, and use this mixture to see how many drops can be added to the second penny before it overflows. Which penny held more drops of water?

Variation

Test other coins to see how many drops of water a quarter, nickel or a dime can hold. Make a chart to keep track of your results.

Floating Orange

Simplicity Level:

Do oranges float or sink? What about if you remove the skin? The answer might surprise you. In this experiment, you'll learn about the concept of buoyancy and why oranges float or sink.

Materials

- 1 clear vase or glass large enough to fit 3 oranges
- Water
- 3 oranges or clementines

Directions

Fill the vase three-quarters full of water. Drop 1 orange with its skin on into the vase. You'll notice the orange floats on top of the water. Remove the skin from a second orange and drop it into the water. Does it float or sink? You will notice it now sinks even though it's lighter with the skin removed. Finally, peel the third orange, but leave the skin on around the top of the orange. Drop this orange into the water. It should sink, but not all the way.

Variation

Use a lemon and then a lime for this experiment. Do they work the same way?

The Hows and Whys

The orange with the skin floats because the skin of the orange is porous and holds a lot of air. (There's also some air trapped inside the orange.) Buoyancy is the ability of an object to float in water, air or another liquid. Therefore, the orange with the skin still on is buoyant in water. The skin acts like a life vest for the orange! Once the skin is removed, all that air in the skin and inside the orange is gone and it sinks to the bottom. When you leave the top part of the orange skin on the orange, some of the air is still trapped inside the orange and there are some air bubbles in the skin, so the orange "floats" in-between the top and bottom of the water.

OCEAN IN A JAR

SIMPLICITY LEVEL:

In this experiment, you'll make an ocean in a jar and also learn about why oil and water don't mix.

MATERIALS

- 1 clear jar with a lid that seals tightly
- Water
- Blue liquid food coloring
- Baby oil or vegetable oil
- Pecan
- Superglue (optional)

DIRECTIONS

Fill the jar halfway with water and add a few drops of blue food coloring. Mix in the food coloring by placing the lid on the jar and shaking. Open the jar and fill it the rest of the way with the oil. Add the pecan. Place the lid on the jar, and if you want, you can use the superglue to prevent it from opening. Turn the jar on its side, and watch the blue ocean waves move back and forth as you move the jar. Notice the pecan stays between the oil and water.

THE HOWS AND WHYS

Oil and water don't mix because water is made up of polar molecules and oil is made up of nonpolar molecules. Water is held together by molecules that have a positive charge on one end and a negative charge on the other end. Oil molecules are evenly balanced and the charge is evenly dispersed. This means that oil molecules are more attracted to other oil molecules and water molecules are more attracted to other water molecules. Therefore, water and oil never mix. The two liquids are said to be immiscible. But why does the pecan float between the water and oil? This is because the pecan is less dense than water but denser than oil, so it stays suspended right in-between the two liquids.

VARIATIONS

Add other objects to your ocean to see if they float or sink. Also, to make a lava lamp, add an effervescent antacid tablet to the mixture. Remove a bit of oil before doing this so it doesn't overflow.

CHAPTER 2

SOLIDS

Solids are objects that have a definite shape and volume. They retain their shape even when not confined by another object. Their particles are stable and typically packed together more closely than liquids or gases. In this chapter, you will do experiments involving solids and explore concepts that include static electricity, heat transfer, inertia and magnetism.

Growing Crystals

Simplicity Level:

In this fun activity, you're going to grow your own colorful crystals!

Materials

- Water (see Note)
- Saucepan
- Epsom salt (see Note)
- Wooden spoon
- Several clear jars
- Liquid food coloring
- Large salt crystals or pebbles

Note: You will need equal parts hot water and Epsom salt for this experiment. Start with 1 cup (240 ml) of water and 1 cup (400 g) of Epsom salt. If you have smaller jars, start with ½ cup (120 ml and 200 g) of each. You may need a little extra Epsom salt.

Directions

Ask a grown-up to heat the water in the saucepan until the water is hot but not boiling. Add an equal amount of Epsom salt into the saucepan and mix thoroughly with the wooden spoon. If you find all the Epsom salt absorbs into the water, add some more. You should see some extra salt on the bottom of the saucepan. Have your grown-up pour the mixture into the jars, and add 10 drops of food coloring (a different color in each jar). Add the large salt crystals to each of the jars. This will help to start the crystals forming. Place the jars in the refrigerator overnight to allow the crystals time to form. The next day, remove the jars from the refrigerator and pour out any excess liquid to reveal your beautiful crystals! Keep your crystals dry and they will last for a long time!

The Hows and Whys

Epsom salt is also known as magnesium sulfate. Hot water absorbs more salt than cold water, so when you added Epsom salt to hot water, you created a supersaturated solution. Then, when you cooled the mixture in the refrigerator, the water could no longer hold all the salt, so the magnesium sulfate pulled away, creating all the crystals!

Variation

Remove some of your crystals from the jar and examine how they look and feel. How easily do they break? Add some of them to water to see what happens. Do they absorb into the water or stay intact as solid crystals?

How Strong Is an Eggshell?

SIMPLICITY LEVEL:

Eggshells are actually much stronger than you would think. In this easy experiment, we'll test how strong an eggshell is and whether or not you can break it just by squeezing it with your hand.

Materials
- 1 raw egg
- Small ziplock bag (see Note)

Note: You can do this experiment without the ziplock bag, but it may get a little messy.

Directions
Place the egg in the ziplock bag. Make sure all the air is out of the bag and zip it shut. Place the egg squarely in the palm of your hand and with your fingers around the egg, squeeze as hard as you can. Did it break? If you're squeezing evenly around the egg, it shouldn't.

The Hows and Whys

The egg does not break because the strength of an eggshell lies in its shape. It resembles a three-dimensional arc, which is one of the strongest architectural forms. The curved form of the eggshell distributes pressure evenly all over the entire egg, rather than at one point. When you try squeezing around the entire egg, you are distributing pressure around the entire egg, and it is very hard to break the shell. If you poke an egg with a finger, the egg will crack because the pressure will be placed on that one specific spot on the egg. This is why eggs won't break when a hen sits on it but will break when a baby chick pecks at it with its beak.

Variation

If you want to get messy, squeeze the egg with a ring on and note how it breaks much easier.

TEAR THE PAPER

SIMPLICITY LEVEL:

Did you know paper tears easily in only one direction? It's true! In this experiment you'll test that theory and learn why this happens.

MATERIALS
- Construction paper

DIRECTIONS

Hold a piece of construction paper vertically, and tear it directly down the middle. Notice how it tears in a straight line. Hold a second piece of paper horizontally. Try tearing it down the middle. Notice that it tears at an angle. Try again with the smaller torn pieces and see if you get the same result.

THE HOWS AND WHYS

Have you ever looked at a piece of wood? If you have, you probably noticed the grain of the wood flows in one direction. Because paper is made of wood, it also has a grain that flows in one direction. If you tear the paper along that grain, it tears straight and evenly, but if you go against the grain, it tears at an angle.

VARIATION

Fold the pieces of construction paper. Do they fold easier horizontally or vertically? It should be easier to fold along the grain.

Straw in a Potato

Simplicity Level: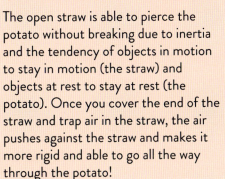

Think you can push a paper straw through a potato? At first glance it wouldn't seem like a straw could go through a potato without getting destroyed, but you'd be surprised how simple it actually is!

The Hows and Whys

The open straw is able to pierce the potato without breaking due to inertia and the tendency of objects in motion to stay in motion (the straw) and objects at rest to stay at rest (the potato). Once you cover the end of the straw and trap air in the straw, the air pushes against the straw and makes it more rigid and able to go all the way through the potato!

Materials

- Paper straw
- Raw potato

Directions

Hold the straw firmly and stab it into the potato. You will see that the straw pierces the potato a little bit. Flip the straw over and cover the end with your finger. Stab the potato. Be sure to hold the potato in a way that you won't stab yourself with the straw as it moves through the potato. If you're using a paper straw as instructed, the end you already stabbed into the potato becomes somewhat wet and weakened. When you switch to the other end, you should be able to get the straw all the way through!

Variations

If you're having any trouble piercing the potato, soak the potato in water for 30 minutes first. Also, try this experiment with other fruits and vegetables you have around the house.

One-Sided Paper: Möbius Strip

SIMPLICITY LEVEL:

Have you ever heard of a one-sided piece of paper? Probably not. But by making something called a Möbius strip, you're going to create your own one-sided piece of paper. And to prove it, you'll draw a single line that covers the whole piece of paper without picking up your pencil!

Materials
- Scissors
- Paper
- Tape
- Pencil

Directions

Cut a long, rectangular shape from the paper that's 1 inch (2.5 cm) wide. Place the ends of the rectangle end to end. Give one of the ends a half twist so the top of one end faces the bottom of the other end. Tape the ends together to form a loop. With the pencil, draw a straight line along the center of the strip. Keep drawing until you reach the starting point of your line. Take a look at the strip and notice that both sides have a line down the center even though you never picked up your pencil! You've made a one-sided piece of paper!

The Hows and Whys

A Möbius strip is a surface with only one side. When you drew the center line, it traveled twice the length of the paper to complete the loop. We use Möbius strips in places such as conveyor belts, computer printer ribbons and continuous-loop recording tapes.

Variations

Cut your Möbius strip down the center line you drew. What happens? You get one long strip with two full twists in it instead of two separate strips! Also, remake your one-sided paper and cut the Möbius strip one-third from the edge of the paper. What happens? You get a large, thin loop and a smaller, thicker loop that are linked!

Spinning Eggs

SIMPLICITY LEVEL:

Did you know that you can tell the difference between a raw egg and a hard-boiled egg just by giving them a spin? In this experiment, you will learn about inertia and be able to show your friends this fun trick!

Materials
- 1 hard-boiled egg
- 1 raw egg

Directions
Place both eggs on their sides on a flat surface. Give the hard-boiled egg a spin. While it is still spinning, place your finger on it to stop it, and then remove your finger. Notice how it stops moving. Give the raw egg a spin. While it is still spinning, place your finger on it to stop it. Remove your finger. Notice how the raw egg starts spinning slowly after you release your finger. This is how you can tell the difference between the raw egg and the hard-boiled egg!

The Hows and Whys
Because the hard-boiled egg is solid inside, it acts as one solid, and when the egg is stopped the entire egg comes to a stop. The raw egg is liquid inside, so when the hard shell is stopped from moving, the interior liquid keeps moving and causes the egg to keep spinning once your finger is lifted. This tendency of objects in motion to stay in motion is called inertia.

Variation
Spin both eggs at the same time and see which one spins faster. Show a friend this trick and see if they can figure out which egg is raw and which is cooked.

Make a Copper-Plated Nail

Simplicity Level:

In this experiment, you're going to use a pile of pennies to make a copper-plated nail!

Materials
- ½ cup (120 ml) lemon juice or vinegar
- Small bowl
- 10–15 copper pennies (dull coloring, made before 1985)
- Pinch of salt
- 2 steel nails (cleaned)

Directions
Add the lemon juice to the bowl. Place the pennies in the bowl, and stir in the salt. Let the pennies rest for 10 minutes. Add one of the nails to the bowl for 15 minutes. Remove the nail and compare it to the other nail. It's changed to a copper-plated nail! If nothing has changed, try soaking the nail overnight.

The Hows and Whys
The copper in the pennies reacts with the acid of the lemon juice or vinegar to form a new compound called copper citrate. When you add the nail to the bowl, the copper citrate attaches to the nail, forming a thin layer of copper on the nail. This layer is permanent and cannot be removed!

Variation
Dip a nail halfway in the solution to coat only half of the nail.

Banana Secret Message

Simplicity Level:

Want to send a secret message to your friend? Here's a fun way to do it using only a banana and a toothpick.

Materials
- Banana (unpeeled)
- Toothpick

Directions
Lay the banana on its side and locate its largest, flattest area. This will be the best place to write your message. Use the toothpick to make small holes in the banana peel in the shape of letters. At first, you won't be able to read the message, but if you wait 1 hour or longer, you'll see your message darken on the banana peel, and your message will be readable!

The Hows and Whys
When the banana peel gets punctured or damaged, the pigments of the peel turn brown. This is due to a chemical called polyphenol oxidase that is released by the cells of the peel. It reacts with oxygen by turning brown.

Variations
Decorate the banana using this method to tap out various patterns and shapes all over the peel. If you don't have a toothpick, use your fingernail! Write a kind message to a friend or parent and give it to them as a surprise! Experiment to see if the bananas with messages on them ripen faster than bananas without messages on them.

Spinning Forks

SIMPLICITY LEVEL:

Did you know you can make two forks balance on a water bottle with just a quarter? It seems impossible, but by using the center of gravity, it can be done!

Materials
- 1 quarter
- 2 forks
- 1 full plastic water bottle with lid on

Directions
Place the quarter in the center slots of the 2 forks so they are held tightly in place and are facing each other (as pictured). Balance the quarter on its tip on the lid of the water bottle. You will find the quarter stands on its tip quite easily. Try spinning the forks and watch how they revolve around the bottle!

The Hows and Whys
The quarter balances easily on the water bottle because the center of gravity of the forks/quarter is at the tip of the quarter that is touching the water bottle. The center of gravity of an object is the point at which all sides are in balance and all weight is evenly distributed. Objects with a lower center of gravity are harder to tip over (like a race car), whereas an object with a high center of gravity (like a double-decker bus) tips over more easily.

Variation
Find other objects around the house to balance and find their centers of gravity. For example, balance a pencil on your finger to find its center of gravity.

Balancing Can

Simplicity Level:

This fun experiment is also a cool trick that will amaze your friends. You'll learn how to balance a soda can at a 45-degree angle and spin it at that angle!

Materials

- 1 empty soda can
- 2 tbsp (30 ml) water, plus more as needed

Directions

Try balancing the can on the little grooved edge just above the bottom of the can. You will find that you cannot do it and the can tips over. Add 2 tablespoons (30 ml) of the water to the empty can. Can sizes vary, so you will have to try it out and see if you need more water. Tilt the can on its groove so that it's at a 45-degree angle again. I would suggest doing this over the kitchen sink in case the can tips over. Remove your hand and see if it stays balanced without being held up. If it tips over, add a bit more water and try again. Eventually, you will reach a point where the can will stay balanced on its edge. Once you have the right amount of water in the can, gently give the can a push and watch it spin in a circle along the grooved edge while it stays at a 45-degree angle!

The Hows and Whys

The reason the can stays balanced at the 45-degree angle has to do with the can's center of gravity. When the can was empty, the center of gravity was somewhere in the center of the can, and because you had it at an angle, it fell over. When you added water, it shifted the center of gravity to wherever most of the water was. So, when you placed the can at an angle, the water shifted and allowed the can to stay at the angle.

Magic Twirling Paper

Simplicity Level:

Here's a fun way to make paper twirl by just holding your hands near it!

The Hows and Whys

The paper spins because of the heat permeating off your hands. Hot air rises, and the heat from your hands heats the air around the paper. This rising warm air causes the balancing paper to spin.

Variations

Hold your hands below and above the paper to see if it affects the spinning. Also, try holding only one hand on the side of the paper to see what happens.

Materials

- Playdough
- Sharpened pencil with eraser
- Straight pin
- Ruler
- 1 (3 x 3" [8 x 8-cm]) square of tissue paper

Directions

Form a ball of playdough that's 1 to 2 inches (2.5 to 5 cm) thick and stick it to a table. Poke the sharpened end of the pencil into the top of the playdough ball so that it stands straight up. Stick the sharp end of the straight pin into the eraser of the pencil so that it stands straight up with the dull end on top. Fold the square of tissue paper diagonally. Unfold so it has one diagonal line down the middle and refold diagonally in the other direction so that two intersecting diagonal lines are formed on the paper. Place the paper on top of the straight pin so that the intersecting point of the folds is right on the pin. The paper should balance on the pin and look a little like an umbrella. Hold your hands on either side of the paper without touching it and watch the paper slowly spin. If the paper doesn't spin, heat up your hands by blowing on them or washing them in warm water.

Sprouts in a Bag

SIMPLICITY LEVEL:

Plants start out as seeds, and in this experiment, you'll take some seeds (or beans) and watch them sprout into plants!

Materials

- Bowl
- Water
- 5–10 dried lima, pinto, black or kidney beans
- Paper towel
- Ziplock bag
- Tape

Directions

Fill the bowl with water. Place the beans in the bowl and soak them overnight. This warms them up and gets them ready to sprout. Soak the paper towel in water, fold it up and place it in the ziplock bag. Place the beans in the bag on one side of the paper towel. Seal the bag and tape it to a sunny window with the beans facing you (so you can watch them grow). Within 24 hours, you should see the beans start to sprout, and within a week, you should see some nice growth. If your paper towel becomes dry, add more water. Once you see leaves start to form on the sprouts, it is time to move them to a planter with some dirt.

The Hows and Whys

Dried beans are actually seeds that contain a baby plant inside. Germination is the process a plant goes through to grow from a seed. Seeds need special conditions to tell them to start growing. Those conditions include light, air, water and temperature. When all those conditions are optimal, the seed will start to grow. When you gave your seed water and put it in a bright window with a little air, you gave it all the right conditions to start growing into a plant.

Variation

Use several types of beans in different bags and see which ones sprout and grow the fastest. Make a drawing each day of your sprouts to track their growth.

Pencils through a Baggie

Simplicity Level:

Get ready to amaze your friends by making a leak-proof bag that you can stick pencils all the way through without water leaking out! Seems unbelievable, but the power of polymers makes it possible!

The Hows and Whys

The bag doesn't leak water when the pencils puncture it because the bag is made of a polymer. Polymers are made of long chains of flexible molecules. When a pencil is poked through the bag, the flexible molecules move to allow the pencil to pass through and then form a seal around the pencil. Once the pencil is removed, the seal is broken and the water comes pouring out!

Variation

Experiment with different plastic bags you find around the house. Just be sure to do this over a sink or tray in case you get a leak!

Materials

- Ziplock bag
- Water
- Liquid food coloring (optional)
- 5–6 pencils
- Large glass baking dish or pan

Directions

Fill the ziplock bag three-quarters full of water. Add a few drops of your favorite food coloring to make the water a fun color. Don't worry if you don't have any food coloring as this step is totally optional. Seal the bag so no water comes out. Poke one of the pencils all the way through the plastic bag so it is sticking out the other side of the bag. Notice how no water leaked out when you punctured the bag! Repeat with the rest of the pencils. For safety, be sure to keep your hands away from where the sharpened end of the pencil will poke through the bag. After all the pencils have been poked into the bag, place the bag over the large dish (or the sink) and start removing the pencils, one by one. Notice how the water now leaks out of the holes in the bag.

Standing on Eggs

Simplicity Level:

Did you know that eggshells are so strong that you can stand on them without breaking them? Seems too good to be true, but it isn't! In this experiment, you'll learn just how strong an eggshell is and why it's so strong.

Materials

- 24 raw eggs in 2 egg cartons

Directions

Remove your shoes and place the egg cartons side by side on a flat surface. The next step is to stand on the eggs. This works best if you have a helper or two who can hold your hands and get you up onto the eggs very gently. The goal is to disperse the weight across your feet and not apply lots of pressure to one spot. Once your friends have helped you up onto the eggs and you feel steady, have them let go of your hands, and you will find yourself standing on eggs!

The Hows and Whys

Eggshells need to be strong enough so a hen can sit on them but weak enough so a baby chick can peck its way out. The arched design of the egg allows for a large force or weight (like a hen) to be absorbed by the shell without it breaking. But if a strong, pointed force hits the egg (like a peck from a chick) the egg will crack. The arched architecture of the egg is similar to the arches used in making bridges and buildings to support large structures.

Variation

If you don't mind breaking the eggs, try this experiment using a shoe with a heel on it or soccer cleats.

Inertia Checkers

Simplicity Level:

In this experiment, you'll examine Newton's first law of motion, which states that an object in motion tends to stay in motion, and that an object at rest tends to stay at rest. And all we need are some checkers to do it!

Materials

- 10 checkers game pieces

Directions

Build a stack of 9 game pieces. Place the remaining piece 1 inch (2.5 cm) away from the stack. Give the single game piece a strong flick with your finger toward the stack of checkers so that it hits the bottom checker. What happens? Did the bottom checker in the stack fly out of the stack, leaving the rest of the checker stack intact? If so, then you've done the experiment correctly!

The Hows and Whys

The bottom game piece flew out of the stack, leaving the others intact, because of inertia. The entire stack was at rest, and it will stay that way unless a force is applied to it. Because the force of the single checker hitting the stack was only felt by the bottom checker, that checker moved, but left the other checkers in the stack.

Variations

Aim the game piece to hit higher in the stack to see if one higher up will come out in the same way as the bottom one. Make a stack of something that has more friction or stickiness such as a stack of gummy candy rings. Does the experiment work in the same way?

Separating Salt and Pepper

Simplicity Level:

If you had a mixture of salt and pepper, how would you separate them? Would it take you a long time? In this experiment, you will use the power of static electricity to easily separate the salt from the pepper using just a plastic spoon.

Materials

- 1 tbsp (18 g) table salt
- 1 tsp pepper
- Shallow plate
- 1 plastic spoon, fork or comb
- Wool shirt or cloth (optional)

Directions

Place the salt and pepper on the plate and mix them together. Rub the plastic spoon on your hair or a wool shirt or cloth. Hold the plastic spoon near the salt and pepper mix and watch what happens. The pepper jumps onto the spoon, separating itself from the salt!

Variation

Use other spices from your spice cabinet to see if they will be attracted to the negatively charged spoon.

The Hows and Whys

The pepper flakes jump onto the spoon due to static electricity and the fact that the pepper flakes are lighter than the salt crystals. Before you rubbed the comb, it had a neutral charge like most objects. After you rubbed the spoon on your hair or the cloth, you gave it a negative charge because some of the negative electrons from the cloth jumped onto the spoon. This made it ready to attract an object with a positive charge. Pepper flakes are neutrally charged, but pepper polarizes easily, and that means that the negative electrons move to one end of the pepper flakes and the positive electrons are on the other end. So the positive end is attracted to the spoon when it's negatively charged. This is why the pepper flakes moved to the spoon. Salt crystals don't polarize easily, so they stay in place on the plate.

Floating Heart

Simplicity Level:

In this experiment, you'll use the power of magnetism to get a heart to float in the air!

The Hows and Whys

The heart floats due to the magnetic attraction of the magnet and the paper clip. Because the heart is made of tissue paper, it is very light, and the force of magnetism is greater than the force of gravity that is trying to pull the heart to the ground.

Variations

Use different types of paper to make your heart and see if it still floats. Also, make other fun shapes to float!

Materials

- Scissors
- Tissue paper
- Paper clip
- Glue stick
- 1 (24" [61-cm]) piece of thread
- Tape
- Magnet

Directions

Use the scissors to cut a pair of 1- to 1½-inch (2.5- to 4-cm)-wide hearts out of the tissue paper. Place 1 heart on a flat surface and place the paper clip in the center of the heart so that a small bit of the paper clip is sticking out below the bottom of the heart. Use the glue stick to glue the second heart on top of the first. Make sure the paper clip in-between them is sticking out of the bottom a bit. Lace the thread through the paper clip and tape the ends of the thread to a table or other flat surface. Pick up the heart and place the magnet just above the heart to keep it floating in the air. The magnet shouldn't be touching the heart but sitting just above it so that the heart floats with nothing touching it but the string.

WALL MARBLE RUN

SIMPLICITY LEVEL:

Here's a fun way to use recycled materials and the power of gravity to make a marble run!

MATERIALS

- Recycled materials such as empty paper towel rolls, small boxes, newspaper, small fruit baskets, etc.
- Scissors
- Painter's or masking tape
- 1 marble

DIRECTIONS

Gather your recycled materials near the wall you want to build on. Cut the paper towel rolls in half so they are open semicircles. This will give you twice as much track for your marble run. Open both ends of any small boxes to use as tunnels. Next, use the painter's tape to stick the tubes and boxes on the wall. Start from the top and work your way down. If you have a small fruit basket, you can tape it to your last tube to catch the marble. (You can also just place it on the floor.) Once you've completed the marble run, test it out to see if your marble makes it all the way through and lands in the basket. If it doesn't make it, adjust your marble run and test it again!

THE HOWS AND WHYS

The marble moves through the marble run from top to bottom due to gravity. Gravity is a force that pulls objects toward each other. Earth's gravity is what keeps you on the ground and not floating around in space. The force of gravity also keeps all the planets in our solar system rotating around the sun!

VARIATIONS

Use other recycled materials you find around your home to add even more obstacles to your maze! Also, place a spoon at the end of one of your tunnels to make the marble jump to the next part of the maze.

Ice Tunnels

SIMPLICITY LEVEL:

Get ready to make cool, colorful ice tunnels inside a block of ice!

The Hows and Whys

Salt lowers the freezing point of ice, so areas of the ice mounds that had more salt on them started to melt more quickly, allowing tunnels and pathways to form.

Materials

- 2 bowls
- Water
- Glass baking dish
- Salt
- Several small clear drinking glasses
- Liquid food coloring
- Dropper or pipette

Directions

Fill the bowls three-quarters full of water and place them in the freezer. Once the water has frozen, remove them from the freezer, turn them upside down and place the ice in the glass dish. (You may need to run the bowls under warm water for a few seconds to loosen the ice.) Sprinkle a generous amount of salt onto each ice mound. Fill the drinking glasses with water and add a few drops of different colors of food coloring to each glass. Use the dropper to add colored water to your ice mounds. As you add the colored water, the ice will start cracking, and tunnels and pathways will form in the ice. Because the water is colored, you can see the tunnels making their way through the ice. Using different colors helps to see the pathways mix and form new colors!

Variation

Make different-shaped ice creations by using beach toys or other containers. Do the tunnels form differently for these different shapes?

Ice Cream in a Bag

Simplicity Level:

Making ice cream at home is not difficult! In this experiment you will make homemade ice cream using only a ziplock bag and a few ingredients!

Materials

- 4–6 cups (460–842 g) ice
- ⅓ cup (77 g) coarse salt
- 1 (1-gallon [3.8-L]) ziplock freezer bag
- 1 cup (240 ml) heavy cream
- 1 tsp vanilla extract
- 2 tbsp (30 g) sugar, or to taste
- 1 (1-qt [960-ml]) ziplock freezer bag
- Gloves (optional)

Directions

Add the ice and salt to the gallon-sized (3.8-L) ziplock freezer bag. Add the cream, vanilla and sugar to the smaller ziplock bag. Remove as much air as possible and seal the bag. Mix the ingredients inside the sealed bag using your hands. Add the smaller, sealed bag with the cream, sugar and vanilla to the larger bag. Seal the larger bag and shake until its contents are frozen. This should take 5 to 10 minutes, depending on how hard you shake it. You may want to wear a pair of gloves if the bag gets too cold to handle. Open both bags to reveal your homemade ice cream in the inner bag!

The Hows and Whys

Salt lowers the temperature at which water freezes. As you are shaking, you will notice the ice start to melt as it is mixed with the salt. This surrounds the ice cream mixture with really cold water and helps it freeze faster as you are shaking it around! This is the same reason we add salt to icy roads and walkways in the wintertime. The salt causes the ice to melt so it's not slippery when we walk or drive on the winter roads.

Variation

Make flavored ice cream by adding fresh fruit, crumbled cookies or sprinkles!

Straw Wrapper Worms

Simplicity Level:

Worms are normally found outside, but here's a fun way to make your own worms at the kitchen table or a restaurant!

Materials
- Straw with a wrapper (see Note)
- Water
- Dropper or pipette

Note: You can find wrapped straws at most coffee shops and restaurants.

Directions
Carefully scrunch the wrapper on the straw from both ends so that it's all bunched up in the middle of the straw. Carefully slide the bunched-up wrapper off the straw and set it on the table. Add water to the dropper and add a few drops of water to your bunched-up straw wrapper. As you add water, your "worm" will start to wiggle and squirm and grow!

The Hows and Whys

The straw wrapper "worm" starts to move and grow when water is added due to capillary action. As water is added to the wrapper, it moves through the tiny fibers of the paper. (This is similar to how a plant absorbs water from its roots and distributes it to the rest of the plant.) As the paper absorbs the water, it starts to grow, straighten out and return to its original shape.

Variation

Add color to your straw wrapper with washable markers before scrunching it up to make colorful worms!

BLUE COINS

SIMPLICITY LEVEL:

Vinegar is sometimes known as a household cleaner, but what happens if you don't wipe it off what you're cleaning? Well, if you're cleaning your coins, they may just turn blue!

MATERIALS
- 2 paper towels
- Plate or small tray
- Nickels and dimes
- Vinegar

DIRECTIONS

Place 1 paper towel on the plate, and then place the coins on the paper towel. Pour a small amount of vinegar on the coins. The paper towel should be wet underneath the coins. Cover the coins with the second paper towel, and pour some more vinegar over that so it's wet on every part that covers the coins. Leave the plate sitting for 24 hours. Remove the paper towel and examine your coins.

THE HOWS AND WHYS

Nickels and dimes both contain copper. If vinegar is allowed to sit on copper, it begins to turn blueish-green, and it gives the coins a blueish-green color called verdigris. Verdigris is a blueish-green patina that forms on metals containing copper.

VARIATIONS

Keep soaking the coins beyond the 24 hours to see if more blueish-green color develops. Test other coins to see if they change as well.

Balancing Forks

Simplicity Level:

In this experiment, you'll use a toothpick to balance two forks off the side of a cup. It won't make sense to your eyes, but once you understand how the center of gravity works, you can show your friends and amaze them!

Materials
- 2 forks
- 1 toothpick
- 1 clear drinking glass

Directions
Hold the forks facing each other and interlace them by their prongs. Find the point where they balance on a finger without falling. This is their center of gravity. Insert a toothpick into this point on the forks and balance the toothpick on the edge of the glass. It may take a few tries to find the right point, but once you find it, the toothpick and forks will balance, horizontally, off the edge of the glass.

The Hows and Whys

The forks appear to balance off the side of the glass due to their center of gravity. The center of gravity of an object is the point where the entire weight of an object is concentrated so that if you support that point, you can support the entire object. When you joined the forks together, they became one object, and their center shifted from their individual centers of gravity to one at the point where you were able to balance them on your fingertip. Then, when the toothpick was added and the new object was turned on its side, the center of gravity shifted again to a point just below where the toothpick balanced along the glass.

Variation

You'll need an adult's help for this variation. Light the toothpick end inside the glass on fire. You'll find the toothpick stops burning at the point where it hits the glass (due to it cooling off), and the structure stays intact. Also, light the outside of the toothpick structure. You'll find the same thing happens once the flame hits the forks.

Coin in the Bottle

SIMPLICITY LEVEL:

In this experiment, you'll use the power of inertia to get a coin into a bottle without touching it!

The Hows and Whys

The coin stays in place while the paper moves due to inertia. Inertia is the tendency of an object in motion to stay in motion and an object at rest to stay at rest. When you flicked the cardstock, it set it in motion, but the coin stayed in place. Once the coin was over the empty bottle, gravity took over and caused it to fall into the bottle.

Materials

- 1 (3 x 3" [8 x 8–cm]) piece of cardstock or cereal box
- 1 empty clear water bottle with a small opening
- 1 coin, smaller than the mouth of the bottle

Directions

Place the paper square over the opening of the bottle, and then set the coin on top of the paper square just over the opening of the bottle. Give the edge of the square a good flick with your finger so it flies off the bottle horizontally. If you flick it just right, you'll find that the cardstock moves but the coin stays in place and drops directly into the bottle!

Variation

Use other objects such as a marble. Do some items work better than others?

Notepad Friction

SIMPLICITY LEVEL:

Here's a fun way to get two notepads to stick together using only the power of friction!

Materials
- 2 notebooks of the same size

Directions

Open both notebooks to the last page or back cover. Lay one back cover over the other back cover. Next, alternate laying one page from each notebook over the other so that the notebooks become interlaced. Be sure to keep the pages flat as you do this. Once all the pages are interlaced, fold the covers over each other. Get a partner, if you can, or use both hands to hold each of the edges of both notebooks and try to pull them apart. You'll find that as hard as you try, it's impossible to pull them apart!

The Hows and Whys

The notebooks appear to be stuck together because as you apply a force when trying to pull them apart, the normal force between all the pages increases, and this increases the overall friction, making the pages very difficult to pull apart.

Variations

Use notepads of different sizes. Does it still work? Then, try only doing half of the pages. Can you pull them apart?

Balloon Skewers

Simplicity Level:

You probably think that by sticking a balloon with a sharp object you would pop it, right? Well in this experiment, you will use the properties of polymers to pierce a balloon with a skewer without popping it!

Materials

- Latex balloon
- Wooden skewer

Directions

Inflate the balloon until it's three-quarters full and tie it off. You do not want to overinflate the balloon. Insert the skewer into the balloon, close to the point where you tied the balloon. The skewer should be pointed so that it will exit at the tippy top of the balloon. If done correctly, you will find the skewer pierces both ends of the balloon without popping it! Slowly remove the skewer from the balloon and watch it deflate.

The Hows and Whys

The balloon is made of molecules called polymers. The molecules are long chains, and they have elasticity, which causes the balloon to stretch. The points at the top and bottom of the balloon were stretched the least, so when you inserted the skewer at these points, the molecules were able to move around the skewer while keeping the air inside the balloon. If you had tried to insert the skewer in the middle of the balloon where the molecules were already stretched out, the molecules would not have been able to move and stretch to accommodate the skewer and the balloon would have popped!

Variations

Draw black dots all over another balloon before inflating it. Blow up the balloon three-quarters full and tie it off. Notice how some of the black dots get very large and some stay small. The dots that stay small have the least amount of stress on them and would be able to handle the skewer entering at those points. If you want to try piercing a large black dot, apply a piece of tape to the entry and exit points. The tape will help hold the molecules together and keep the balloon from popping at these high-stress points.

Jumping Shapes

SIMPLICITY LEVEL:

Here you will use the power of static electricity to make paper shapes jump without ever touching them!

MATERIALS
- Tissue paper or regular paper
- Scissors
- Latex balloon

DIRECTIONS

Cut the tissue paper into different shapes. You can make regular shapes such as circles, squares and triangles, or you can do fun shapes like flowers, lightning or animals. Blow up the balloon and tie it off. Rub the balloon on your hair for 30 seconds, and then hold the balloon near the cutout shapes without touching them. Watch the shapes jump up and stick to the balloon! How long do they stay stuck on the balloon?

The Hows and Whys

When you rubbed the balloon on your hair, you created static electricity. This happened because some of the electrons from the neutral balloon transferred to your hair and gave the balloon a negative charge. When the balloon got close to the paper shapes, the shapes were attracted to the balloon and jumped up to stick to it!

Variations

Use different types of paper and different sizes of shapes to see if they stick to the balloon as easily. Also, try rubbing the balloon longer on your hair or on a wool sweater to see if the shapes stick to the balloon longer.

Spin a Penny in a Balloon

Simplicity Level:

Harness the power of centripetal force to get a penny spinning inside a balloon with just a few quick flicks of your wrist!

Materials
- 1 penny
- Latex balloon (white or clear if possible, but any color will work)

Directions

Insert the penny into the uninflated balloon so it falls to the bottom. Blow up the balloon halfway to three-quarters full, and tie it off. Hold the balloon from the tied end and twirl it. At first, the penny will flop around the balloon all wacky, but soon it will start to move in a circular motion along its side. At this point, stop spinning the balloon and just watch the penny twirl around and around. It will slowly make its way to the bottom of the balloon and stop spinning. At this point, give it another twirl and start the process all over again. Notice the sound the penny makes while it is swirling around and around the balloon.

The Hows and Whys

Because the balloon is circular in shape, it forces the penny to move in a circular motion. When you provided the force to get the penny moving, it quickly took the shape of the circle and started to go around and around. The force that kept the penny moving in a circle is called centripetal force. This is the same force that keeps the Earth moving around due to the pull of the Sun's gravity.

Variations

Use different sizes of coins and balloons to see how it changes how long the coin spins and the sounds it makes. Also, try using an object such as a hex nut or something that's not smooth.

Spinning Pencil

SIMPLICITY LEVEL:

In this fun experiment, you'll make a pencil spin on top of a water bottle without ever touching it!

Materials

- Pencil
- 1 full water bottle with cap
- Latex balloon

Directions

Balance the pencil on its side on top of the water bottle. Blow up the balloon and tie it off. Rub the balloon on your hair, and then hold the balloon near the end of the pencil (but not touching it). Watch as the pencil starts to move toward the balloon!

The Hows and Whys

When you rubbed the balloon on your hair, some negative electrons jumped from your hair to the balloon, giving it a negative charge. When you held the negatively charged balloon near the pencil, the pencil moved toward the balloon. This is because the pencil has a slightly positive charge. In science, opposite charges attract, so the pencil was attracted and drawn to the balloon.

Variations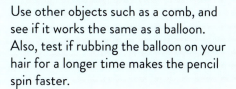

Use other objects such as a comb, and see if it works the same as a balloon. Also, test if rubbing the balloon on your hair for a longer time makes the pencil spin faster.

Turn Milk into Plastic

Simplicity Level:

Did you know you can turn a plain old glass of milk into plastic by adding just one ingredient? It sounds unbelievable, but it's true!

Materials
- 2 cups (480 ml) milk
- Saucepan
- 2½ tbsp (38 ml) white vinegar
- Bowl
- Spoon
- Paper towels
- Liquid food coloring (optional)
- Cookie- or dough-cutters (optional)

Directions

Add the milk to the saucepan, and have an adult help you heat the milk on the stove until it starts to steam. Remove the pot from the heat. Add the vinegar to the bowl, and then pour the hot milk into the bowl. Mix with the spoon. You will see white clumps start to form. Keep mixing. Once the mixture has cooled a bit, lay 3 to 4 layers of paper towels on a table or countertop. Use the spoon to remove the white clumps (curds) and place them on a paper towel. Fold the paper towel edges over to dry off the curds and remove excess liquid. If you want to make your plastic a different color, add a few drops of food coloring to the curds and mix together with your fingers. If you want to make shapes, you can use cookie-cutters or just mold different shapes with your fingers. You should be able to mold the curds for 1 hour. After you have molded the curds to their desired shape, set them aside to dry for 2 days.

The Hows and Whys

When hot milk is mixed with the acidic vinegar, it makes the casein molecules in the milk reorganize and form a long chain. This created the white clumps you saw. These clumps or curds are called casein plastic. This type of plastic was used to make things such as buttons, ornaments and brush sets back in the early 1900s.

Variation

Add glitter or other decorative items to your plastic to make even more elaborate creations!

Floating Drawings

Simplicity Level:

Want to see your drawings float on water? Well, you can in this simple experiment!

Materials
- Dry-erase markers (new ones work best)
- Glass baking dish
- Warm water

Directions

Use the markers to draw simple shapes on the glass dish. You can make stick figures, flowers, hearts or any shape you want! Try to keep the shape connected from start to end. After the drawings dry, gently pour some warm water over the drawings and watch them float to the top and dance around the surface of the water! Gently blow on the drawings to move them around.

The Hows and Whys

Dry-erase marker ink is made of alcohol and a release agent made of silicone oils. When you write with the marker, the alcohol dries up, leaving just the release agent. When the water hits the silicone oil, it repels it, and because it is less dense than the water, it floats to the top!

Variations

Turn a floating drawing into a temporary tattoo by dipping your hand or arm onto one of the drawings. When you pick up your hand, the drawing will be on it! Let it dry and you have a tattoo! Another fun variation is to draw a long, swirly line and then erase it by picking it up out of the water when it's floating! It will lift out of the water like a string!

Clean the Pennies

Simplicity Level:

You've probably noticed that pennies can be bright and shiny or dull and dark. In this experiment, you'll learn how to clean pennies to make them all bright and shiny!

Materials

- Several dull pennies
- Small bowl
- Vinegar
- Salt
- 1 tsp water
- Paper towel

Directions

Place the pennies in the bowl. Hold 1 dull penny aside so you can see how much you were able to clean the others. Pour enough vinegar into the bowl so that it covers the pennies. Sprinkle some salt into the bowl, and then add the water. Swirl the solution around so that the salt absorbs into the mixture. You will immediately start to notice your pennies getting brighter. Leave them in the solution for 5 minutes, and then rinse them off and rub them dry with the paper towel. Your dull, dark pennies are bright and shiny and like new!

The Hows and Whys

Over time, pennies oxidize and become dull and dirty-looking. When vinegar and salt combine, they form a weak solution of hydrochloric acid, which is a solution that cleans metals such as copper.

Variation

Use other household items to clean pennies such as ketchup, hot sauce, lemon juice, milk or dish soap. Do they work as well as the vinegar-and-salt combo?

Fluffy Slime

Simplicity Level:

Slime is such a fun thing to stretch, squish and play with, and fluffy slime is even stretchier, squishier and more fun to play with!

The Hows and Whys

Slime is both a polymer and a non-Newtonian fluid. Non-Newtonian fluids behave very differently than normal fluids. As you apply pressure to them, they harden, and when you let them sit, they turn back into a liquid. With slime, if you pull on it very fast, it will break, but if you stretch it slowly, it pulls apart into long strings. Fluffy slime is fluffy from all the air bubbles in the shaving cream.

Materials

- Bowl
- 1 (5-oz [147-ml]) tube white school glue
- 2 tbsp (30 ml) water
- ½ tsp baking soda
- Spoon
- 2 cups (500 ml) shaving cream (not the gel kind)
- Liquid food coloring (optional)
- 1–2 tbsp (15–30 ml) contact solution (must contain boric acid or sodium borate)
- Oil or lotion (optional)

Directions

In the bowl, add the glue, water and baking soda. Mix with the spoon, and then add the shaving cream and mix. Add a few drops of food coloring in your color of choice or leave it white to make white slime. Add 1 tablespoon (15 ml) of contact solution and continue to mix. You will notice the consistency of the slime start to change, and it will look more like slime. Keep mixing and adding contact solution as you mix. Once the slime starts to separate from the sides of the bowl, pick it up and knead it with your hands. This slime is a bit messy and it takes a few minutes of kneading to get it to fully form. You can put oil or lotion on your hands to help the slime stick less.

Continue to add small amounts of contact solution until the slime is not sticky at all, but be careful not to add too much or the slime will not be as stretchy. Once the slime is complete and you're done playing with it, store it in an airtight container. It will keep for at least 1 week. The fluffiness will only last a day or so as the shaving cream settles, so it will just feel like regular slime as it ages. Also note that slime does stick to clothing, so if you happen to get it on your clothes, pour some vinegar on the spot and rub it in. The slime will dissipate and come right off.

Variation

Insert the end of a straw in your slime and blow to form a slime bubble!

Oobleck

Simplicity Level:

Oobleck is one of the coolest substances in the world. It acts like a liquid when it is sitting at rest, but it behaves like a solid when pressure is applied to it. Most important, it is super fun to play with, so let's make some!

Materials
- Bowl
- 1 cup (128 g) cornstarch
- ½ cup (120 ml) water
- Spoon
- Liquid food coloring (optional)

Directions

In the bowl, add the cornstarch and water. Use the spoon to mix them together. You can make more or less than this, but use the proportion of 2:1 cornstarch to water. You'll notice that you have to mix slowly or else the mixture gets very hard. You can add a few drops of food coloring to make your oobleck colorful, but this step is optional. Once the color is mixed in (if using), pick up a ball of the liquid and roll it in your hands. You will notice you are able to roll it into a solid ball. Then, let the ball sit in the palm of your hand. You will see the ball melt back into a pile of liquid.

The Hows and Whys

Oobleck is a non-Newtonian fluid. This means it behaves like a liquid when left alone but as stress is applied to it, it changes viscosity. Viscosity is a fluid's measure of its resistance to flow. For example, water has a low viscosity because it flows very easily, and syrup has a high viscosity because it flows very slowly and it's thick. In the case of oobleck, when you applied stress to the oobleck by rolling it in your hand, you turned it into a solid. But as soon as you let it sit in the palm of your hand and no stress was applied to it, it turned back into a liquid.

Variation

Add a little more water to your oobleck to make a great sidewalk paint. Take it outside and make some art on your driveway!

Rubber Egg

Simplicity Level:

Did you know it's possible to make a raw egg bounce without breaking it?

Materials
- 1 raw egg
- 1 clear drinking glass or jar
- White vinegar
- Liquid food coloring (optional)
- Small plate
- Glass baking dish

Directions
Carefully place the egg in the glass. Pour in enough white vinegar to cover the egg completely. If you want to make your bouncy egg colorful, add a few drops of food coloring. Cover the glass with the small plate and place in the refrigerator for 3 days. Remove the egg and rinse it gently under water. You will notice a film start to come off (formerly the eggshell) and reveal the translucent membrane underneath. If you added liquid food coloring to your mixture, the membrane will be this color. This membrane is soft, and you can lightly squeeze it without breaking it.

Place the glass dish on the countertop, and bounce the egg 1 to 2 inches (2.5 to 5 cm) above the dish. Watch it bounce and roll around without breaking. After you've fully examined the egg and are ready to get messy, hold the egg a little higher over the dish to see if it bounces or breaks. How high can you hold it before it breaks when you drop it?

The Hows and Whys
When you placed the egg in vinegar, a chemical reaction took place between the eggshell and the vinegar. Eggshells are made of calcium carbonate, and vinegar is an acid. The acid in the vinegar breaks up the calcium and the carbonate and dissolves the eggshell. You may even have seen some small bubbles forming on the eggshell when the vinegar was added. The bubbles are actually carbon dioxide gas.

Variation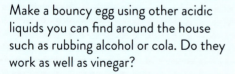
Make a bouncy egg using other acidic liquids you can find around the house such as rubbing alcohol or cola. Do they work as well as vinegar?

Craft Stick Explosion

Simplicity Level:

Here, you will utilize the power of potential energy and kinetic energy to create a craft stick explosion just by weaving the sticks in a very specific way!

The Hows and Whys

Potential energy is stored energy. As you wove together the craft sticks, you created more and more potential energy in the chain as the sticks were bent over and under each other. The sticks want to return to their normal, straight position, so slightly bending them creates this energy. When you let go of the last stick, all the potential energy that has been stored up is converted to kinetic energy and the chain explodes!

Materials

- 20 or more (6" [15-cm]) jumbo craft sticks in 2 different colors (see Note)

Note: It's easier to use just 2 colors when learning how to make the chain. Once you get the hang of it, you can use more colors.

Directions

Make an X shape with 1 stick of each color. Take a stick of the same color as the one on the bottom of the X and place one end of the third stick under the bottom of the first stick. Have the middle of the third stick cross over the second stick so that it's on top of the second stick, but the head of the third stick is under the first stick. The fourth stick should be the same color as your second stick. Place the fourth stick in an X on top of the third stick, and place the end under the open end of the first stick. The fourth stick should be parallel to the second stick of the same color. Place the fifth stick (same color as the third stick) in an X pattern over the fourth stick, and place the end under the second stick. The fifth stick should be the same color as and run parallel to the third stick.

Repeat the pattern with the remaining craft sticks. Be sure to hold down the sticks as you add more, otherwise the explosion will happen before you are ready! Once you've used all your craft sticks, let the end go and watch the chain explode and the sticks fly in the air! If you don't want the sticks to explode right when you let them go, you can tuck the end of the last stick placed under the open end of the same color stick. This means both ends of the last stick placed are tucked under other sticks. This will hold the chain in place until you remove that last stick.

VARIATION

Once you've mastered making a two-color chain, use lots of colors to make your explosion really colorful!

Floating Ring

Simplicity Level:

In this amazing experiment, you're going to make a plastic ring magically float above a balloon!

Materials

- Thin plastic bag (such as a produce bag or animal waste bag)
- Scissors
- Balloon
- Towel or sweater

Directions

Place the plastic bag flat on a table and cut a 1-inch (2.5-cm) strip across the middle of the bag so you are left with a 1-inch (2.5-cm)-thick ring. Blow up the balloon and tie it off. Rub the balloon with the towel for 30 seconds. Then, rub the towel on the piece of plastic for 30 seconds. Finally, hold the plastic ring 6 to 12 inches (15 to 30 cm) over the balloon, and watch as it levitates!

Variation

Find other light objects (like a feather) around your house to levitate.

The Hows and Whys

This plastic ring levitates over the balloon due to the power of static electricity. When you rubbed the towel on the balloon and on the plastic ring, you gave each of them a negative charge. Then, when you placed the ring over the balloon, they repelled each other with their negative charges, so the ring appeared to be levitating above the balloon. If both objects have the same charge, they repel and try to get away from each other. On the other hand, if two objects have opposite charges, they attract. For example, if you've ever rubbed a balloon on your hair, you've seen that your hair sticks to the balloon. This is because when you rubbed the balloon on your hair, the balloon became negatively charged and your hair became positively charged.

Egg Drop

SIMPLICITY LEVEL:

In this experiment, you will drop a raw egg into a glass of water without ever touching it!

MATERIALS

- 1 clear drinking glass
- Water
- Plastic plate or metal pie pan
- Empty toilet paper or paper towel roll
- 1 raw egg

DIRECTIONS

Fill the glass three-quarters full of water. Place the plate on the center of the top of the glass. Then, place the paper roll directly over the glass in the center of the plate. Finally, place the raw egg on top of the paper roll. If your egg falls through the paper roll, you need to find a larger egg or a smaller paper roll. Now for the fun part! Use your dominant hand to hit the edge of the plate and make it horizontally fly off the glass. You will want the paper tube to fall over, so you need to hit the plate with enough force to make that happen. You may want to do a couple of practice tries before adding the egg. Once you have the motion down, add the egg and try it again. If you do it correctly, the egg will fall directly into the glass of water!

THE HOWS AND WHYS

Newton's first law of motion states that an object in motion tends to stay in motion, and an object at rest tends to stay at rest. When you hit the plate away from the glass, it moved away, but the egg was at rest and it stayed at rest. Once nothing was left to hold the egg in place, gravity took over and the egg fell into the glass.

VARIATIONS

Use an orange or ping pong ball instead of the egg. Also, try using glasses and plates of different sizes. Does it change how you do the experiment?

Potato Skewer Balance

Simplicity Level:

In this experiment, you will be able to balance a potato on the tip of a wooden skewer. It sounds impossible, but it's actually quite easy, and you'll also make a very pretty spinning sculpture!

Materials
- Several wooden skewers, with 1 cut in half
- 1 small potato
- 1 full, unopened plastic water bottle
- Grapes or carrot slices

Directions

Stick one of the cut skewer pieces into the potato with the pointy tip sticking out. Try to balance the pointy end of the skewer on the top of the water bottle. It's impossible, right? Next, place 2 skewers evenly and pointed down on either side of the potato. Stick grapes onto the pointy ends of these skewers. Try balancing the potato on the tip of the skewer half. Then, stick more wooden skewers into the potato, and stick the grapes onto the ends sticking out. After adding each skewer, check to see if the potato balances. You may have to make some adjustments by moving the skewers or the grapes, but it should balance. Continue adding skewers that stick out in all directions. You should end up with quite a beautiful sculpture. Try spinning it!

The Hows and Whys

The center of mass of an object is the point where an object's mass is concentrated. If you balance an object at its center of mass, it won't tip one way or another. When the potato just had one skewer through it, the center of mass was somewhere in the center of the potato, and it was very hard to balance it. When you added additional skewers, the center of mass shifted to somewhere underneath the potato, and it became much easier to balance the entire object (including the skewers).

Variation

Find other objects (or pieces of fruit) to add to your sculpture.

Whip Off the Napkin

Simplicity Level:

Have you ever seen someone pull a tablecloth off a table full of dishes without any of the dishes moving or breaking? In this experiment, you will do something similar with a napkin and a cup!

Materials

- Napkin or paper towel
- Plastic cup
- Water (optional)

Directions

Place the napkin on a table or countertop with half on the table and half off the table. Place the empty cup (or add some water if you dare) on the napkin part that is on the table. With a quick motion, pull down on the napkin part hanging off the table. If you did the motion fast enough, the cup should stay standing on the table! If the cup falls, try again with a quicker motion.

The Hows and Whys

The cup stays standing on the table due to inertia and Newton's first law of motion. This law states that objects at rest tend to stay and rest, and objects in motion tend to stay in motion. Because the cup was at rest, it wanted to stay at rest unless a force acted on it. The napkin moving under the cup did not provide enough force or friction to cause the cup to move or fall off the table.

Variations

Use other objects such as a small bowl or plate and repeat the experiment. Also, use a silicone hot pad instead of a napkin. What happens?

Melting Ice with Pressure

Simplicity Level:

Did you know you can melt ice just by applying pressure to it?

The Hows and Whys

When you applied pressure to the ice cube, you caused heat energy to form, and this energy started to melt the ice on top of the ice cube. You can even see the lines where the fork was touching the ice cube because of the pressure applied and the heat it generated.

Materials

- 2 ice cubes
- 2 paper plates
- 1 metal fork

Directions

Place each ice cube on a separate paper plate. Keep the plates in the same area so you know the temperature and conditions are the same for each. Apply pressure to the top of one of the ice cubes with the fork for 3 minutes. The grooves on the fork should be pressed against the top of the ice cube, and you should not be touching the ice cube with your free hand. You may hear the ice crack a bit after applying pressure. After 3 minutes, remove the fork and compare the ice cubes. You will find the untouched ice cube unmelted and the ice cube you applied pressure to has started melting. You will also be able to see groove marks where the fork was pressing on the ice cube.

Chapter 3

GASES

In the previous chapters, you learned about solids, where atoms are packed close together, and liquids, where atoms are spread out a bit more. In this chapter, you'll learn about gases, where the atoms are very spread out! You are surrounded by gases. From the air you breathe (oxygen) and the air you exhale or bubbles in a can of soda (carbon dioxide) to the air that makes a balloon float (helium), different gases are all around us. In these experiments, you'll learn about air pressure as well as do some experiments to show you how gases are all around you, even if you can't see them!

Smoking Bubbles

Simplicity Level:

If you ever receive dry ice in a shipment, do NOT throw it away! Use it to make bubbles that appear to have smoke inside them! But be sure to have a grown-up help you handle the dry ice as it can be dangerous if touched with your hands!

The Hows and Whys

Dry ice might be one of the coolest substances on Earth. It is the solid form of carbon dioxide frozen to -109.3°F (-78.5°C), and it is mostly used as a cooling agent. It is so cold that it can cause frostbite if touched. The coolest thing about dry ice is that when it melts, it turns into a gas and evaporates, so there is no water left over. The smoke or fog that forms is caused by the dry ice rapidly warming and is a mixture of carbon dioxide gas and water vapor. Adding soap to the dry ice causes the smoke to get trapped in the bubbles, creating a cool effect when the bubbles pop!

Materials

- 1 clear vase
- Warm water
- Dish soap
- Tongs
- Dry ice (for grown-ups to use; see Note)

Note: Do not touch the dry ice or you can burn yourself!

Directions

Fill the vase two-thirds full of warm water. Add a squirt of dish soap. Have an adult use the tongs to pick up a piece of dry ice and drop it into the water and soap mixture. Watch as the dry ice bubbles in the water and soap bubbles start to form. Reach in and collect some bubbles. Pop them and watch as smoke from the dry ice floats out of the bubbles, creating a cool and creepy effect! When the bubbles stop forming, add another piece of dry ice and watch the reaction happen all over again!

Dry Paper Experiment

SIMPLICITY LEVEL:

In this experiment, you're going to submerge a piece of paper in water, but it's going to stay totally dry! Sounds impossible, right? It's totally possible using the properties of air!

Materials

- 1 large clear vase
- Water
- Piece of paper or paper towel
- 1 small clear drinking glass

Directions

Fill the vase halfway with water. Crumple the piece of paper and place it in the bottom of the small glass. Turn the glass upside down, and make sure the paper stays at the bottom. Submerge the glass upside down into the vase of water so that the piece of paper in the glass is below the water line. Lift the glass out of the water and examine the piece of paper. It stayed totally dry!

The Hows and Whys

When you submerged the upside-down glass into the water, there was air inside the glass that stayed trapped in the glass and prevented water from getting in. Air takes up space and is lighter than water, and because there was nowhere for the air to go, it stayed in place and protected the paper.

Variation

Tip the glass over a bit in the water and see what happens. Does the air slip out? Does the paper get wet?

Fill the Balloon

SIMPLICITY LEVEL:

Did you know that hot air and cold air take up different amounts of space? It's true! This simple experiment demonstrates the space air molecules take up as they are heated and cooled.

The Hows and Whys

As air molecules get hot, they move around more and occupy more space, thus inflating the balloon. When the balloon was moved to the ice water, the molecules cooled off, moved closer together and occupied less space.

Variation

Fill two tall jars with water (one hot and one cold), and then add a few drops of blue food coloring to the cold jar and red food coloring to the hot jar. Notice which color mixes first. Which color do you think will mix quicker? Why?

Materials

- Very hot water
- 2 glass baking dishes
- Cold water (including ice)
- Balloon
- 1 empty plastic 2-L bottle

Directions

Get a grown-up to help you pour the very hot water into one of the glass dishes until it's halfway full. Add the cold water with ice to the other baking dish until it's halfway full. Place the end of the balloon over the opening of the 2-liter bottle. Place the bottle in the hot water and watch the balloon inflate. Then, move the bottle to the cold water and watch it deflate. Repeat these steps to watch the balloon inflate and deflate.

Lifting with Air

Simplicity Level:

Have you ever wondered how birds and airplanes fly? In this fun experiment, you will use the same idea to lift a piece of paper using only air.

Materials

- Thin strip of paper or dollar bill

Directions

Hold the paper with both hands on one of the shorter sides. Hold that short side up to your mouth so that the rest of the paper is hanging down in front of your mouth (kind of like a long tongue). Blow on the top edge of the paper so that all the air you're blowing goes on top of the paper. What happens? Amazingly, the paper lifts up and sticks straight out!

The Hows and Whys

When you blew across the top of the paper, you lowered the air pressure on top of the paper, which made the air pressure under the paper higher, causing it to lift up! This is a great demonstration of Bernoulli's principle, which states that the faster air flows over a surface, the less it pushes on that surface, therefore lowering the air pressure on that surface. This is the reason why birds and planes can fly. The air rushing over the curved wings of birds and planes is lower than the air pressure on their undersides. This gives them the upward force they need to soar!

Variation

Another fun way to demonstrate Bernoulli's principle is to face a hair dryer up to the sky, turn it on and add a ping pong ball to the stream of air. You will find the ball stays within the stream of air and doesn't fall. This is because the stream of air is lower in air pressure than the air outside the stream. So the ball is held in place whenever it tries to leave the stream.

Diving Ketchup Packet

Simplicity Level:

Do you think it's possible to move a ketchup packet up and down in a bottle of water without touching it? Well it is! All you need is a little squeeze.

Materials

- 1 ketchup packet
- Bowl
- Water
- 1 empty clear 1-L water bottle with cap

Directions

Check that your ketchup packet floats by placing it in a bowl of water. If it sinks, you will need to find another packet that floats. Fill the bottle all the way to the top with water. Add the ketchup packet. If you need to add a bit more water to fill the bottle to the brim, do that now. Screw the cap on tightly. Squeeze the bottle and watch the packet sink to the bottom of the bottle. Let go and watch the packet rise to the top!

The Hows and Whys

There is actually a tiny air bubble in the ketchup packet, which is what caused it to float in water. When you squeezed the bottle, it caused that air bubble to condense (as gases condense easier than liquids) and get smaller. This made the entire ketchup packet denser than the water, so it sunk to the bottom of the bottle. When you let go of the bottle, the air expanded and got less dense, so the ketchup packet floated back to the top.

Variation

Squeeze the bottle just hard enough so that the ketchup packet sits in the middle.

Blow Paper in a Bottle

Simplicity Level:

In this experiment, you'll try to blow a paper ball into a bottle with a straw. Sounds simple enough, but you'll find that no matter how hard you huff and puff, the paper just won't go in!

Materials

- 1 empty plastic 1-L bottle
- Small ball of paper that fits loosely in the bottle opening
- Straw

Directions

Lay the plastic bottle on its side on a counter or table. Place the ball of paper so that it sits loosely right inside the mouth of the bottle. Use the straw to blow air directly into the opening of the bottle. You will find that the paper moves around a bit, but then it suddenly pops out of the bottle opening instead of going into it!

The Hows and Whys

You might think the bottle looks empty, but it's actually full of air. When you blew more air at the bottle through the straw, there was nowhere for the air to go because the bottle was already full of air. Much of the air you blew actually went along the outside of the bottle. This created an area of low pressure outside the bottle, which caused the paper to pop out!

Don't Open the Bottle

SIMPLICITY LEVEL:

Here, you'll use air pressure and surface tension to create a fun trick to play on your friends and family!

The Hows and Whys

The water stays in the bottle because when the cap is on there is no air pressure pushing on the water inside forcing it to come out of the holes. And surface tension plays a part in allowing the water itself to stop up the tiny holes. The water molecules stick together and form a type of "skin." Once the lid is removed, air pushes the water out of the little holes.

Materials

- 1 empty clear 1-L water bottle (or similar size) with cap
- Water
- Permanent marker
- Pushpin

Directions

Fill the water bottle to the top with water. Screw the cap on tightly. Remove the label from the bottle, if necessary, and write with the marker on the front of the bottle, "Don't Open." Use the pushpin to poke small holes 1 to 2 inches (2.5 to 5 cm) from the bottom of the bottle and all the way around it. You should have 8 to 10 holes in the bottle when you are done. You may see a drop or two of water come out, but the rest of the water will stay in the bottle. Set the bottle somewhere a friend or family member will see it. When they open the bottle, water will start to flow out of all those holes! When they pick up the bottle, some drops may come out of the holes, but it will really start flowing once they remove the cap!

Exploding Baggie

Simplicity Level:

This experiment is a fun twist on the classic baking soda and vinegar chemical reaction. In this version, you will make a ziplock bag explode!

The Hows and Whys

When you mix vinegar and baking soda, a chemical reaction occurs and carbon dioxide gas is created. The bag starts filling up with the carbon dioxide gas, and when the bag is full of gas and can't hold any more, it explodes!

Variations

Add food coloring to the vinegar for a colorful explosion. Also, try playing with different amounts of vinegar and baking soda to see if it changes the time it takes for the bag to explode.

Materials

- ½ cup (120 ml) vinegar
- Sandwich-size ziplock bag
- 1 tbsp (14 g) baking soda
- ¼ piece of a paper towel

Directions

This is a messy experiment, so head outside! Add the vinegar to the plastic bag. Close the bag and set it aside. Place the baking soda into the center of the paper towel piece, and wrap up the edges of the paper towel so the baking powder is folded into the center. Open the bag, drop the paper towel into the bag and seal it immediately. Set the bag on the ground and watch as the vinegar and baking soda start to mix. You'll see the bag fill with air and get very full. Keep watching and listening and soon you'll hear a pop and see the bag explode!

DIY Fire Extinguisher

Simplicity Level:

Did you know you can make a fire extinguisher at home using baking soda and vinegar? It's true! Because we're dealing with fire in this experiment, you'll need a grown-up to help you.

Materials

- 2 tbsp (28 g) baking soda
- 1 clear drinking glass or jar
- Vinegar
- Candle
- A match or lighter (for grown-ups to use)

Directions

Add the baking soda to the glass. Add the vinegar until the glass is half full. Have a grown-up help you light the candle. Once the fizzing in the glass has come down a bit, tilt the cup slightly over the flame like you're pouring air over the flame. Watch as the flame goes out!

The Hows and Whys

Real fire extinguishers use chemicals and carbon dioxide to put out fires. When you combined baking soda and vinegar, carbon dioxide gas was created. Carbon dioxide is heavier than oxygen, so when you hold it over a flame, it replaces the oxygen around the flame. Because carbon dioxide is invisible, you didn't see anything pouring out of the glass, but when you held it over the flame, you could tell it was there. The flame needs oxygen to continue burning, and without it, the flame went out.

Variation

Light multiple candles (with a grown-up) and see if you can extinguish more than one flame.

Soda Volcano

Simplicity Level:

This experiment is one of the funnest and messiest in this book, but it's a must-try! You're going to make a volcano that shoots high up in the sky with just two ingredients: soda and mints!

Materials

- 1 full 2-L bottle of diet soda (see Note)
- Piece of paper
- Tape
- Index card or small piece of cardstock
- 1 (1.3-oz [38-g]) pack of Mentos® mints

Note: Diet soda works best and is less messy and sticky, but any type of carbonated soda will work.

Directions

This is a messy experiment, so head outside and find a wide-open space you don't mind getting a little messy. Open the bottle of soda and place it on the ground where you want your volcano to erupt. Roll a piece of paper into a long tube the same size as the roll of Mentos and tape it so it doesn't fall apart. Place the index card over one end of the paper tube and add 7 to 10 Mentos into the tube. Finally, place the index card over the opening of the soda bottle and be sure the tube of Mentos is directly above the soda bottle opening. With a quick motion, remove the index card so the Mentos can all fall into the soda quickly, and then move away from the soda bottle. The eruption will happen instantly, and you will get wet if you don't make a run for it!

The Hows and Whys

The bottle of soda contains lots of carbon dioxide bubbles. You may have noticed when you drop something in a glass of soda, bubbles attach to it and are removed from the soda. The same thing happens when you drop the Mentos into the soda. What makes the mints so different and special is that they have tiny pits all over their surface, so there are lots of places for the carbon dioxide bubbles to attach to. The mints also sink to the bottom of the bottle, so when they are added, they sink to the bottom and produce so many gas bubbles that all the liquid flies out of the bottle to make room for all the carbon dioxide bubbles that just formed.

Variations

Do this experiment again, but change the amount of Mentos you drop in. You can also test different types of soda to see which ones give the biggest eruption. Also, test whether or not it makes a difference if the soda is warm or cold.

Can Crusher

Simplicity Level:

There are lots of ways to crush a can, but in this fun experiment, you will use sudden temperature changes to make the can implode! Be sure to have a grown-up handy to help you with this one, as you will need to use the stove.

Materials
- Small bowl
- Cold water
- Ice cubes
- 1 empty soda can
- Saucepan
- Tongs

Directions

Fill the bowl with cold water and a couple of ice cubes. You want the water to be very cold. Add enough water to the soda can to cover its bottom (1 to 2 tablespoons [15 to 30 ml]). Place the can in the saucepan and place the pan on a stove burner. Have your grown-up turn on the burner. Listen until you hear the water in the can start to bubble and boil. Keep heating the can for 1 minute longer. Next, have your grown-up turn off the burner and use the tongs to pick up the can. Move the can above the bowl of cold water, turn it upside down and plunge it into the cold water. What happens? The can implodes once it touches the cold water!

The Hows and Whys

When you heated up the water in the can, the water became water vapor that replaced a lot of the air in the can. When you removed the can from the heat, turned it upside down and plunged it into cold water, the water vapor that was in the can turned back into water. Because the can was upside down, no new air could get into the can to replace the water vapor. Without air inside the can to push back on the can, the outside air pressure was too strong and it crushed the can!

Lemon Volcano

Simplicity Level: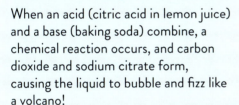

Did you know you can make a volcano using a lemon? In this experiment, you will use lemons (an acid) and baking soda (a base) to make lemon volcanoes!

The Hows and Whys

When an acid (citric acid in lemon juice) and a base (baking soda) combine, a chemical reaction occurs, and carbon dioxide and sodium citrate form, causing the liquid to bubble and fizz like a volcano!

Materials

- 2 or more lemons
- Knife (for grown-ups to use)
- Glass baking dish
- Liquid food coloring
- Dish soap
- Baking soda
- Craft stick or fork

Directions

Have a grown-up cut off the ends of the lemons so they will stand up in the baking dish. Then have them cut the lemons in half. Place the lemon halves in the baking dish with the middle of the lemons facing upward. Add a few drops of food coloring to the lemons in whatever color you want your volcanoes to be. Add a small squirt of dish soap to each lemon half, and sprinkle the baking soda over them. To activate the volcanoes, take a craft stick and stab it into each lemon half a few times. Watch as the lemons start to fizz and bubble!

Variations

Use other citrus fruits such as a lime or orange to make a volcano. Do they work as well as the lemon?

Aluminum Foil Boat

SIMPLICITY LEVEL:

Have you ever wondered why boats float in the water even though they're heavy and filled with items that sink? In this experiment, you will learn about gravitational forces and buoyancy forces and their relationship in keeping a boat afloat! You'll also build your own boat and see how many coins it can hold before sinking.

Materials
- 1 bin that can hold 6" (15 cm) water or a bathtub
- Water
- 1 (10 x 12" [25 x 30–cm]) piece of aluminum foil
- 40–50 coins

Directions
Fill the bin with 6 inches (15 cm) of water. Fold the aluminum foil into the shape of a boat. Your boat can be any kind of shape, and as big or small as you want, as long as it floats in the water. Set the boat in the water to see if it floats. If it does, start adding coins—one at a time—and see how many coins your boat can hold before it sinks. If you are doing this challenge with a friend, make sure you both use the same type of coins. Keep adding coins until the boat sinks.

The Hows and Whys

When a boat is in the water, it floats because the gravitational force pushing down on the boat is less than the upward force (called buoyancy) that is calculated by how much water is displaced by the boat. Because a solid object, such as a rock, doesn't displace any water, it sinks to the bottom. But a huge ship displaces lots of water, so it is able to float.

Variation

Make another boat with a different shape and see if it can hold more coins. Does it help to have a larger boat with shorter sides or a smaller boat with larger sides?

Dissolving Seashells

Simplicity Level:

Seashells are very hard and take quite a beating as they move through the ocean. But did you know you can make a seashell disappear just by placing it in a jar of vinegar?

Materials
- White vinegar
- 1 clear jar
- 1 seashell (see Note)

Note: Use a seashell that's not too thick or it may take longer to disappear.

Directions
Add enough white vinegar to the jar to submerge the shell. Drop in the seashell. You will immediately notice bubbles forming on the seashell. Check back after 1 day to see if your seashell looks any different. If it is still there, replace the vinegar with new vinegar, and let it sit for another day. Your seashell should be gone!

The Hows and Whys
The seashell didn't actually disappear, but rather, it dissolved in the vinegar. Seashells are made of calcium carbonate (a base), and when they are mixed with vinegar (an acid), they react to produce carbon dioxide (the bubbles you saw).

Variation
Use shells of various thicknesses and colors to see how long they take to dissolve.

Rising Water Candle Experiment

SIMPLICITY LEVEL:

Here's a fun experiment that demonstrates the power of air pressure and how it can move water!

Materials

- ½ cup (120 ml) water
- Large plate
- Liquid food coloring
- Spoon
- Candle
- A match or lighter (for grown-ups to use)
- 1 clear glass jar or beaker

Directions

Add the water to the large plate. Add a couple drops of food coloring to the water. Mix with the spoon so that the water is uniformly colored. Place the candle in the middle of the plate and have a grown-up light the candle. Place the glass jar over the candle and watch what happens. The flame will burn for a bit but then go out when it runs out of oxygen. After the flame goes out, you will notice the colored water rising up inside the jar!

The Hows and Whys

It may seem like the lack of oxygen is what causes the water to rise, but it actually has more to do with temperature. When the candle was lit inside the jar, it heated up the air in the jar, and that air took up more space. You may have noticed some bubbles coming out from the bottom of the jar. Then when the flame was extinguished, the air rapidly cooled off and contracted. Because cool-air molecules move around less than hot-air molecules, they take up less space. When the cool air contracted, the air pressure inside the jar was less than the air pressure outside the jar, so the outside air pushed the water into the jar until the air pressure on both sides of the jar were equal.

Chapter 4

Light, Color & Sound

In this chapter, you will dive into experiments that explore light, color and sound. You'll learn about primary and secondary colors, symmetry, sound waves and ultraviolet rays! You'll also make some beautiful pieces of art along the way! Let's get started!

String Art

SIMPLICITY LEVEL:

Symmetry is when something is exactly the same on both sides of an axis. It's very hard to draw something that has perfect symmetry. Have you ever tried drawing a heart and making it exactly the same on both sides? It is very difficult! But in this activity, you will create beautiful, symmetrical art using string!

Materials
- Liquid food coloring
- Small bowls
- 1 (12" [30-cm]) piece of string or thread (any kind will work, but polyester works best)
- Spoon (optional)
- Rubber glove (optional)
- Sketch pad or several pieces of white paper

Directions
Add various colors of food coloring into the small bowls. Do NOT water down the food coloring or your painting will not be as vibrant. Dip the string in one bowl of food coloring until it is completely immersed. If you use polyester thread, you may need to use a small spoon to help cover the thread, as it will want to sit on the surface. Cotton thread tends to sink right into the color. Lift the string out of the food coloring, and if there is a lot of excess dripping off, take your index finger and thumb (wear the glove if you want to stay clean) and remove some of the excess paint. Lay the string on a piece of paper in the sketch pad. You can swirl it around or make a pattern, but have the end of the string you're holding end at the edge of the paper so you are able to pull out the string. Now close the sketch pad (or lay another piece of paper over the string and paper). Place the palm of your free hand on top of the string-and-paper sandwich you created, and while holding down the paper, pull out the string from between them. Open up the papers to reveal a symmetrical design on both pieces of paper! Repeat this procedure with all the different food coloring "paints" you have made to create a beautiful, symmetrical artwork.

The Hows and Whys
You created a symmetrical work of art because each piece of paper looks like a mirror image of each other. In nature, things such as butterflies, flowers and leaves are symmetrical. Can you find small discrepancies in the images that make them not perfectly symmetrical?

Variation
Experiment with different thicknesses of string and thread and try different types of paints to see how it changes the paintings.

Oil and Water Art

SIMPLICITY LEVEL:

Oil and water don't mix, and in this experiment, you'll use that fact to create some amazing liquid art!

Materials
- Vegetable oil
- Shallow plate
- Water
- 4–5 small bowls
- Liquid food coloring
- Dropper or pipette

Directions
Add just enough vegetable oil to the plate to cover the bottom. Add water to the small bowls until they are half full, and then add various colors of food coloring to the water and mix to create your colors. Use the dropper to add drops of colored water to the plate of oil. Move the dropper around as you're placing drops of colorful water to make different patterns and designs. The drops will stay separate from each other but may start to join as the plate gets fuller. Be sure to take a photo of your final creation!

The Hows and Whys

Because water and oil don't mix, they are said to be immiscible. Water and oil don't mix because water is made up of polar molecules and oil is made up of nonpolar molecules. Polar molecules (for example, water) carry a positive charge on one end and a negative charge on the other end. Water molecules are attracted to each other because the positive end of one molecule is attracted to the negative end of another water molecule. Nonpolar molecules (such as oil) are evenly charged and do not carry a positive or negative charge on either end. Polar molecules and nonpolar molecules do not mix because they are not attracted to each other.

Variation

Use primary colors and get the colored drops to mix to make secondary colors.

Egg Art

SIMPLICITY LEVEL:

Decorating eggs can be more than just dying them solid colors. In this experiment, you'll create personalized art on an egg!

Materials

- 1 white hard-boiled egg, at room temperature
- 1 crayon
- 1 cup (240 ml) warm water
- 1 tbsp (15 ml) vinegar
- Liquid food coloring
- 1 small cup

Directions

Draw a picture on the egg with a crayon. (It helps if the eggs are warm or at room temperature because crayons don't work as well on cold eggs.) Make your egg dye by mixing the water, vinegar and 10 to 15 drops of food coloring in the cup. Place the egg in the dye for 7 to 10 minutes. Remove the egg to reveal your creation! The entire egg should be dyed except for the parts you colored with crayon! Set the egg aside until it is dry.

The Hows and Whys

Crayons are made of an oily wax. Because oil and water don't mix, the eggshell that is covered by the crayon stays protected from the water-based dye and doesn't absorb any color. Oil and water don't mix because water is made up of polar molecules and oil is made up of nonpolar molecules. Water is held together by molecules that have a positive charge on one end and a negative charge on the other end. Oil molecules are evenly balanced, and the charge is evenly dispersed. This means that oil molecules are more attracted to other oil molecules and water molecules are more attracted to other water molecules.

Variation

Write a secret message on an egg in white crayon, and then reveal the messages by dyeing the egg.

Wet and Dry Painting

SIMPLICITY LEVEL:

In this fun activity, you'll examine how color spreads when you paint on a wet or dry canvas. It's also a great lesson on how plants absorb nutrients!

The Hows and Whys

You probably noticed the color spreading much more quickly on the damp paper towel. The color on the dry paper towel spread for a bit, but once it got absorbed by the paper towel, the color stopped spreading. This is similar to how the roots of plants work. When they are in damp soil, they are able to absorb nutrients more easily than in dry soil, and therefore the plants thrive.

Materials

- 2 paper towels
- Water
- Baking sheet
- Tablespoon
- 4–5 small bowls
- Liquid food coloring
- Dropper or pipette

Directions

Dampen one of the paper towels with water. Keep the second one dry. Place the paper towels side-by-side on the baking sheet. Add 1 tablespoon (15 ml) of water to each of the small bowls, and then add several drops of food coloring to each bowl (using different colors for each bowl). Using the dropper, add colored water to each paper towel. If you really want to see the difference between wet versus dry, make the same paint marks on each paper towel. Keep adding colors to both paper towels. What do you notice? Do the colors blend more easily on the dry towel or the wet one?

Magic Milk

SIMPLICITY LEVEL:

In this colorful experiment, you'll learn about surface tension while watching colors magically swirl through milk.

Materials
- Shallow plate
- Whole milk (2% works as well)
- Liquid food coloring
- Dish soap
- Cotton swab or cotton ball

Directions

Fill the plate with ¼ inch (6 mm) of the milk. (Warm the milk in the microwave for 30 seconds if it came straight from the refrigerator.) Using various colors, add 4 to 6 drops of each food coloring to the milk. Add a drop of dish soap to the cotton swab and touch the swab to the milk mixture. Watch the colors instantly start to twirl, swirl and move!

The Hows and Whys

Milk is made up of mostly water, but it also contains proteins, minerals and fats. It has surface tension, like water, and when soap is added to the milk, it breaks the surface tension by breaking the cohesive bonds between the water molecules. The fats in milk are sensitive to changes in the milk, and the soap causes those fat molecules to twist, bend and move in all different directions as their chemical bonds are altered. Because we added color, we can see the colors swirling throughout the mixture as the bonds are broken. Once the soap and fat molecules are all evenly mixed, the swirling stops.

Variations

Use different color variations for various times of the year such as Independence Day (red and blue), Christmas (red and green) or Halloween (orange and black). You can also add cookie-cutters to the milk before adding the color and soap to make fun, swirling shapes. What happens if you use 1-percent or skim milk (less fat)? Is the reaction the same or different? Finally, use cold milk instead of warm milk. Did it change how the colors swirled?

Coffee Filter Chromatography

Simplicity Level:

The color black may seem like it is only one color, but it is actually made up of a combination of different-colored dyes. This simple experiment will show you all the different colors that go into making black.

The Hows and Whys

The separating of colors is called chromatography. The various colors that combine to make black have various weights. The lighter dyes move faster up the coffee filter while the heavier dyes move more slowly up the filter, so you can see each color as they separate.

Variation

Do this experiment with other dark colors such as purple and green.

Materials

- Black non-permanent marker
- 1 white coffee filter
- 1 small clear drinking glass
- Water

Directions

With the black marker, draw and fill in a 1-inch (2.5-cm)-diameter circle in the middle of the coffee filter. Fold the coffee filter in half, and then fold it again so that it looks like a triangle. Fill the glass three-quarters full of water. Place the black tip of the filter in the water so that it touches the water but the top stays dry. Watch as the black marker starts to spread up the coffee filter and different colors start to appear. Once the filter is saturated with water, remove it from the glass and unfold it. Lay it out to dry. What colors are in the center and which ones made it all the way to the edge?

Water Shapes

SIMPLICITY LEVEL:

When you think of water, you don't think of anything sticky, right? Well the fact is, water molecules like to stick together. Using this concept, you're going to create some colorful shapes with water that allow the color to move around.

The Hows and Whys

So why does the colored water only go along the path the clear water creates? Water is made up of one oxygen atom and two hydrogen atoms (H_2O). These atoms have positive and negative charges, which cause them to stick together. Water displays properties of both cohesion and adhesion. Cohesion causes the water molecules to stick to themselves and adhesion causes the molecules to stick to other objects. When clear water is painted on the plate, adhesion causes the water to stick to the plate. When colored water is added to the water on the plate, cohesion causes the water to stick to itself, so it stays on the wet part of the plate and doesn't venture onto the dry part. You will also notice the colored water dome a bit. This is due to surface tension and cohesion because the water molecules are trying to stick together.

Materials

- Tablespoon
- Water
- 4–5 small bowls
- Liquid food coloring
- Paintbrush
- Paper plate
- Dropper or pipette

Directions

Add 1 tablespoon (15 ml) of water to each of the small bowls. Add several drops of food coloring to each bowl (using different colors for each bowl). Make any colors you want or use primary colors (red, yellow and blue) as they will mix well when you add them to your shape. Dip the paintbrush in some clear water and draw a shape on the paper plate. Try a basic shape at first, such as a circle. Use the dropper to add some colored water to the shape. Be sure to drop the colored water onto the line of the shape, and that line should still be wet. You will notice the colored water stays within the wet line you drew on the paper plate. Add another color to the shape using the dropper. Carefully lift up the plate and tilt it slightly back and forth. Notice how the colored water moves around the shape but stays within the lines you drew. The colors will even start to mix if you added more than one color to your shape.

Variations

Fill a glass of water all the way to the top and use a dropper to add more water. Instead of overflowing, the droplets will cause the water to appear to come over the top of the glass.

Fizzy Art

SIMPLICITY LEVEL:

When you combine baking soda (a base) and vinegar (an acid), you get a fun, fizzy reaction. And in this experiment, you'll add color to the mix to make it a fun art project!

MATERIALS
- Baking sheet
- Baking soda
- Tablespoon
- Vinegar
- 4–5 small bowls
- Liquid food coloring
- Dropper or pipette

DIRECTIONS

Fully cover the baking sheet with a layer of baking soda. Add 1 tablespoon (15 ml) of vinegar to each of the small bowls, along with several drops of food coloring (with different colors in each bowl). If you use red, yellow and blue, you can also do some color mixing with the primary colors. Use the dropper to add colored vinegar to the baking soda. Watch as the colors fizz and bubble. Keep adding different colors until all the baking soda has been covered in color. Take a photo of your artwork!

The Hows and Whys

When baking soda and vinegar combine, they produce an acid-base reaction, and carbon dioxide gas is created. Those are the bubbles you see forming. Red, yellow and blue are primary colors, and when you mix them together you can get secondary colors such as orange, green and purple.

Variation

Mix baking soda with your favorite paint, and paint a picture on the baking sheet. Add drops of vinegar and watch the painting fizz and bubble!

Fireworks in a Jar

Simplicity Level:

Fireworks are so much fun to watch! In this experiment, you will make fireworks in a jar! Okay, so they're not really fireworks, but they'll look like bursts of color moving through the water!

Materials
- 1 clear jar
- Water
- Vegetable oil
- Shallow plate
- Liquid food coloring
- Fork

Directions
Fill the jar three-quarters full of water. Pour enough vegetable oil onto the plate to cover it. Add several drops of food coloring to the plate of oil in various colors. The more colors you add, the more colorful your fireworks will be. With the fork, gently move the colors around the oil so that the drops of color break up into smaller drops. Carefully pour the oil and food coloring mixture into the jar of water. At first, you will just see the oil and colors settle on top of the water. But after a few seconds, some of the colorful drops will make their way into the water in tiny bursts and streaks of color!

The Hows and Whys

Oil and water don't mix, and water is heavier than oil, so you probably noticed the oil was sitting on top of the water when you added it to the jar. And because the food coloring is water-based, it did not mix with the oil when it was on the plate. Once you added the oil mixture to the water, the food coloring made its way through the oil and started to mix with the water in beautiful, colorful streaks.

Variations

Change the temperature of the water to see if that affects how the colors mix. Use primary colors for your food coloring and see if you can get the colors to mix once they're added to the water.

Mixing Colors

Simplicity Level:

Here's a fun and mess-free way to mix colors without actually mixing colors!

The Hows and Whys

Red, yellow and blue are primary colors, and when they are mixed with each other, they create secondary colors: orange, green and purple.

Variation

Make more colors such as teal, peach or other, more complex colors. What colors would you need to start with to make these colors? How could you make brown?

Materials

- 3 clear drinking glasses
- Water
- 3 smaller clear drinking glasses that will fit inside the large ones
- Red, yellow and blue liquid food coloring
- Spoon

Directions

Be sure to set up this experiment in a well-lit room as you will want lots of light so you can see the colors well. Fill the larger glasses halfway full of water. Fill the smaller glasses three-quarters full of water. Add a drop of red food coloring to a large and small glass and mix with the spoon. Next, add a drop of yellow food coloring to a large and small glass and mix. Finally, add a drop of blue food coloring to a large and small glass and mix. Place the matching-color small glasses inside the matching-color large glasses. Now for the fun part! Lift the smaller glasses out of their matching colors and move them to colors that don't match. For example, move the small yellow glass into the large red glass. What color does the liquid in the small glass look like now? It should look orange. Now place the small blue glass in the large yellow glass. Does the liquid in the small glass look green? Finally, place the small red glass in the blue liquid. Do you see purple?

Make a Sunset

Simplicity Level:

If you've ever seen a sunset, you've seen the beautiful red, yellow and orange hues. In this experiment, you'll create your own sunset in a jar!

Materials

- 1 clear glass jar or drinking glass
- Water
- 1 tsp or more 2% or whole milk
- Flashlight

Directions

Fill the jar three-quarters full of water. Add a small amount of milk to the water until the water is just murky enough so you can't see through it. Move to a dark room, and shine a flashlight through the side of the jar so it's facing you. You won't see the flashlight, but you'll see light coming straight through the jar at you. What color is that light? You'll notice it's got a yellow/orange hue just like a sunset!

The Hows and Whys

White light from the sun is actually made up of lots of different colors. When the sun starts to set, it has to travel farther through the atmosphere to reach your eyes. When light hits the dust and gases in the atmosphere, it scatters in many directions, and different colors scatter differently. Light waves with shorter wavelengths (blue) scatter the most, while light waves with longer wavelengths (red and orange) scatter the least. In our experiment, the fats and protein molecules in the milk represent all the particles in the atmosphere that scatter the light rays, so when the flashlight is shining through the glass jar, the blue rays scatter, but the red and orange rays make their way through the milk to reach your eyes.

Variation

Shine the flashlight up through the bottom of the jar. When you look at the jar through the side, you will see this light look bluer than when it was shined through the side of the glass. This is because those shorter blue wavelengths are scattering to the sides of the jar and making themselves visible to you.

DIY Rainbow

Simplicity Level:

Isn't it cool when you see a rainbow outside? Usually, if it has been raining and then the sun comes out, for just a few minutes a rainbow will appear. In this experiment, you will create your own rainbow using just a few simple items you have around the house!

Materials
- 1 clear drinking glass
- Water
- 1 small mirror

Directions
Fill the glass three-quarters full of water. Place the mirror inside the glass so that it is tilted at an angle. Angle the glass so that the mirror is reflecting directly at the sun. If you point it at the sun just right, you will see a rainbow appear on your wall! Keep adjusting the angle until a rainbow appears!

The Hows and Whys

White light or sunlight is actually a mixture of all the colors of the rainbow. When light passes through water, the colors are dispersed and reflected back in all the different colors. In real life, a rainbow always appears with the sun behind you. Another cool fact is that the color red has the longest wavelength, so it bends the least and that causes it to be on top of the rainbow arc. Violet has the shortest wavelength, which causes it to bend the most and be at the bottom of the arc.

Variation

Make larger or smaller rainbows by moving the glass closer and farther from the wall.

Playdough Color Mixing

SIMPLICITY LEVEL:

Playdough is a fun, sensory play material, and you can also use it to learn about primary and secondary colors in this color-mixing experiment.

MATERIALS
- Red, blue and yellow playdough

DIRECTIONS
Pinch off a bit of two of the colors (for example, red and yellow) and squish them together. What color do you think will form? Keep squishing and kneading the colors together until you see a new color. Repeat using other color combinations. What happens if you mix all three colors together?

THE HOWS AND WHYS

The color wheel is made up of primary and secondary colors. Primary colors are red, yellow and blue. No colors can combine to make these colors. Secondary colors are orange, green and purple. Primary colors combine to make secondary colors. For example, red and yellow combine to make orange. Yellow and blue combine to make green, and blue and red combine to make purple.

VARIATION

Make a rainbow in playdough with all the colors you've created! Add white and black playdough to your color mixing to make lighter and darker colors such as pink or maroon.

Candy Rainbow

Simplicity Level:

Candy is yummy to eat, but did you know you can use it to make a rainbow? In this experiment, we'll use Skittles® or M&M's® to make a rainbow design.

The Hows and Whys

Skittles and M&M's candies are coated with sugar and dyes. When warm water is added to them, the outer shells start to dissolve, and the colors begin to move into the water and mix with the other colors.

Variations

Make two identical plates of candy and pour ice-cold water on one plate and warm water on the other. What do you notice? Does one plate create the rainbow faster than the other? Also, make different shapes such as a square, triangle or hexagon and see how the colors move on the plate.

Materials
- White plate
- Skittles or M&M's
- Glass of warm water

Directions

Set your plate on a level table or countertop. Arrange your candy on the plate in rainbow-color order around the edge of the plate. Once your candy has made a full circle around the edge of the plate, gently pour the warm water in the center of the plate until all the candy is partially covered. Watch as the colors start to bleed out from the candy and make their way to the center of the plate. If the colors move to one side of the plate, your table is not level. Add something to the bottom of one side of the plate to make it level.

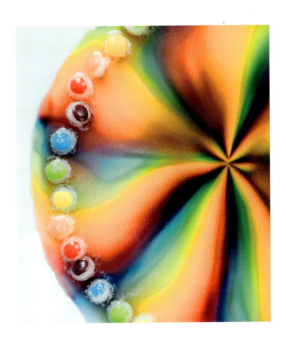

Hot/Cold Watercolor Mixing

Simplicity Level:

As you've seen with some of the other experiments, different liquids have different densities, but water just has one density, right? Well, not exactly. Hot and cold water actually have different densities, and in this color-mixing experiment, you'll see exactly how different they are!

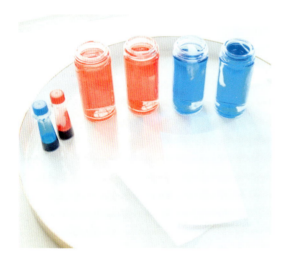

Materials

- 4 small clear drinking glasses
- Baking sheet
- Hot and cold water
- 2 ice cubes
- Red and blue liquid food coloring
- 2 notecards

Directions

Place the glasses on the baking sheet. Fill 2 of the glasses with cold water. Add an ice cube to each to make the water extra cold. Fill the other 2 glasses with hot water. (As hot as the tap water can get from the faucet is fine.) Add red food coloring to the hot glasses and blue food coloring to the cold glasses. Place one of the notecards on top of one of the hot water (red) glasses. Keep your hand on the notecard and flip the glass upside down. Place it directly over one of the cold water (blue) glasses. Remove the notecard so the liquids can mix. Notice how the red liquid stays on top and the blue liquid stays on the bottom. Next, place the second notecard on the remaining cold water (blue) glass. Place your hand on the notecard, flip the glass over and place directly over the remaining hot water (red) glass. Remove the notecard and watch what happens. The liquids mix immediately, turning all the water purple! Finally, flip over the first set of glasses that should still be red and blue and watch them immediately mix and turn purple as well!

THE HOWS AND WHYS

When water is hot, the water molecules are moving around much faster than cold water molecules. This rapid movement creates gaps that make hot water less dense than cold water. When the hot water was on top, it stayed separate from the cold water because it was less dense and stayed floating above the denser cold water. When the hot water was on the bottom and the cold water was on the top, the colors mixed right away because cold water sunk to the bottom and mixed with the hot water.

VARIATION

Try the experiment again using other mixtures of primary colors such as mixing red with yellow and yellow with blue.

Upside-Down Spoon Experiment

Simplicity Level:

Have you ever walked through a fun house and seen those magic mirrors that make you look tall or short or upside down? They're so much fun! Did you know you have a mirror in your kitchen that will make you look upside down?

Materials

- Large, shiny, serving spoon

Directions

Make sure your spoon is nice and shiny so you'll be able to see your reflection in it. You can use any spoon, but a larger one will work better as you will be able to see your reflection better. Hold the spoon up so that you are looking at the inside of the scoop, and examine your reflection. You will see that you and everything around you are upside down! Flip the spoon around so you are looking at the outside of the scoop. Notice everything is right-side-up again!

The Hows and Whys

Light rays always travel in straight lines. When you look in a normal mirror, your reflection travels back to you in straight lines and you get an accurate reflection. When you look into a curved mirror, such as the inside of a spoon scoop, the image gets reversed. That's because the light rays are reflected straight off the curved portions so the top of the image reflects back as the bottom of the image and vice versa, making the image look upside down.

Disappearing Coin

Simplicity Level:

In this easy experiment, you will make a coin disappear simply by placing a glass of water over it!

Materials
- 1 coin
- 1 clear drinking glass
- Water

Directions

Place the coin on a table or countertop. Place the empty glass on top of the coin. Notice how you can still see the coin through the bottom of the glass. Fill the glass with water. If you're looking at the glass from the side, the coin totally disappears! Now, take a peek at the coin by looking inside the glass from the top and you'll see the coin is still there, but it's totally invisible from the side.

The Hows and Whys

Everything we see in the world are light rays that reach our eyes. Light rays travel through the air with very little refraction, so it's easy to see the coin. But when light rays have to travel through water, there is much more refraction (due to molecules being much closer together in water than in air). The light rays bend in the water and none of them are able to reach your eyes, and therefore, the coin looks like it has disappeared.

Variations

Try making different objects disappear under the glass. What happens if you only fill the glass halfway? Does the object still disappear?

Reverse the Image

Simplicity Level:

What if I told you that you could reverse the direction of an arrow just by holding it behind a glass of water? It seems impossible, but it's true!

Materials

- 1 clear drinking glass
- Water
- Marker
- Paper or notecard

Directions

Fill the glass with water. Draw an arrow on the paper. Hold the arrow on the opposite side of the glass of water and observe the arrow through the water. You may need to move it backward and forward from the glass to get the perfect angle, but at the right placement, the arrow will appear to point in the opposite direction! Move the arrow above the water and notice it points back to its original direction.

The Hows and Whys

This amazing optical illusion happens due to refraction or the bending of light. The glass acts as a magnifying glass and magnifies the arrow a bit with the curve of the glass. But once the arrow is held behind the focal point, it reverses itself and the arrow appears to reverse itself. That's why when the arrow is held close to the glass it looks correct, but when you start to move it away from the glass, it suddenly reverses.

Variations

Use different sizes of drinking glasses and see if that affects how far you need to hold the arrow image away from the glass to reverse it.

Water Rainbow

SIMPLICITY LEVEL:

Rainbows are a beautiful phenomenon of nature, but did you know you can easily make a real rainbow in your house with just a glass of water and a sunny window?

MATERIALS

- 1 clear drinking glass
- Water
- White paper

DIRECTIONS

You will need to do this activity on a sunny day. Fill the glass three-quarters full of water. Look for a window in your home where a lot of sunlight shines through. Hold up the glass to the window so that the sun shines through the water. Look around on the floor to spot the rainbow. Then, place the piece of white paper where the rainbow is to really see the colors!

THE HOWS AND WHYS

White light that we get from the sun is actually made of many colors. When white light passes through water, the light rays bend in various directions trying to make their way through the water. This separates them slightly and allows us to see them as a rainbow of colors. Red has the longest wavelengths and is therefore on the outside of the rainbow's arc, while violet has the shortest wavelengths and is therefore on the bottom of the rainbow's arc.

VARIATIONS

See if you can set your glass down and try to color in the rainbow on the white paper as you see it formed! How many colors can you see?

Drawing a Perfect Circle

Simplicity Level:

Try drawing a perfect circle by hand. It seems almost impossible, doesn't it? Here's a simple way to draw a perfect circle using only your hands and a pencil.

Materials
- Paper
- Pencil

Directions

To draw a perfect circle, you first need to locate the little bone at the bottom of your writing hand. Hold your hand palm up and move from your pinky finger all the way to the bottom of your hand. This little bone is located just between where your palm ends and your wrist begins on the pinky side of your hand. Once you find that bone, place it in the middle of the paper and hold the pencil with the tip touching the paper. Now leave that hand perfectly in place and spin the paper with your other hand all the way around until it's back to its original position. (Having a friend move the paper for you can be helpful.) Make sure you leave lots of room on the table to spin the paper so it doesn't run into anything while spinning. Finally, lift the pencil off the paper to reveal the perfect circle!

The Hows and Whys

The bone in your hand acts as a stationary center point for the paper to rotate around as it's turned. Because you are keeping your hand very still and just moving the paper around the center point, you are able to create a perfect circle. It's like making a compass with your hand.

Variations

Make larger or smaller circles by changing the angle you're holding your hand. Try using your non-dominant hand. Is it more difficult?

Ringing Spoon

SIMPLICITY LEVEL:

Here's a fun way to play with sound waves and to make a spoon sound like a ringing church bell!

Materials
- 1 (24" [61-cm]) piece of string
- Teaspoon

Directions
Make an open loop in the middle of the string. Slip the handle of the spoon into the loop and tighten the loop so the spoon stays suspended from the string. Hold each end of the string up to your ears. Plug your ears with your fingers and have each string end between your fingers and your ear. Lightly tap the spoon against a counter, table or another spoon and listen to the sound it makes. It sounds much more like a church bell than a spoon hitting a table!

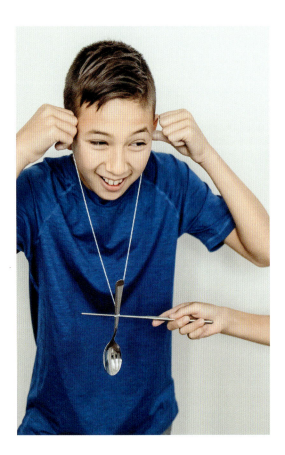

The Hows and Whys
When the spoon hits the table or counter, the string that's attached to the spoon conducts the vibration of the spoon. Those vibrations are sound waves, and the string carries them right up and into your ears.

Variations
Try this same experiment using smaller and larger spoons. How about a fork? Do they make different sounds? Does a larger spoon make a higher or lower sound?

Sun Prints

SIMPLICITY LEVEL:

We all know that the sun emits powerful light rays, but just how strong are those ultraviolet rays? In this experiment, you'll see just how powerful those rays are by how quickly they fade color. And you'll also make some amazing art in the process!

Materials

- Dark-colored construction paper (black, purple, blue, green and red work well)
- Baking sheet
- Interesting shapes such as leaves, branches or flowers
- Small rocks (optional)

Directions

Do this activity on a sunny day that is not too windy. (If it is windy, you can do it indoors in a sunny room next to a window that gives direct sunlight.) Lay the construction paper on the baking sheet. Lay your interesting shapes on top of the construction paper and place the baking sheet directly in the sun. If you are outside, you may want to secure the corners of the paper with small rocks so nothing blows away. After 2 to 3 hours, remove the shapes from the paper. You will notice that any paper that was not covered by a shape faded in the sun, and the areas covered by your shapes are left brightly colored!

The Hows and Whys

The sun emits UV (ultraviolet) light waves down onto the earth, and these waves carry enough energy to break the bonds of some chemicals, such as the dyes in the construction paper. This causes the color in the paper to fade. When the shapes are removed, those parts of the paper remain fully colored because they were protected from the UV light waves. This experiment is a good reminder of why we need to wear sunscreen on sunny days.

Variation

Use magnetic letters or numbers to write out messages or make cards or signs for friends!

Pop a Balloon with a Sun Ray

Simplicity Level:

You are probably already aware of how powerful the sun's rays are, but did you know you can use the rays to pop a balloon?

Materials
- Sunglasses
- Balloon
- Magnifying glass

Directions

Do this activity outside on a very sunny day. Put on the sunglasses and be sure to have a grown-up present to supervise this activity, as the sun's rays are very powerful and could get quite hot. Blow up a balloon until it is very full and tie it off. Stand with your back to the sun and hold the tied end of the balloon with one hand and the magnifying glass with the other. Allow the sun's rays to go through the magnifying glass and onto the balloon. You will see a bright point of light on the balloon (This is why you need to wear sunglasses.) Keep the point of light in one spot on the balloon and pretty soon the balloon will pop!

The Hows and Whys

When the sun's light rays pass through the magnifying glass, the curve of the glass focuses them on a single bright spot. This causes the rubber from the balloon to heat up, weaken and eventually pop!

Variation

Use this same method of harnessing the sun's rays to toast a marshmallow, melt cheese or toast a tortilla chip!

Sound You Can See

Simplicity Level:

Did you know sound actually travels through the air in waves? You can't see the waves, but they are there. In this experiment, you'll set up a contraption that will allow you to see sound in motion!

Materials
- Plastic wrap
- 1 plastic cup
- 1 rubber band
- Black pepper flakes
- Metal pot
- Wooden spoon

Directions
Place a piece of plastic wrap over the opening of the plastic cup, and seal it tightly with the rubber band so that the plastic wrap is flat over the opening of the cup. Add some black pepper flakes to the top of the plastic wrap. Face the opening of the metal pot toward the cup. Bang on the bottom of the pot with the wooden spoon and watch as the pepper flakes bounce around and move each time you bang on the pan!

The Hows and Whys

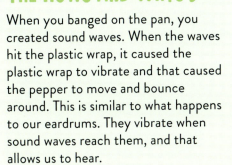

When you banged on the pan, you created sound waves. When the waves hit the plastic wrap, it caused the plastic wrap to vibrate and that caused the pepper to move and bounce around. This is similar to what happens to our eardrums. They vibrate when sound waves reach them, and that allows us to hear.

Variation
Place the cup on top of a speaker or your smartphone and play loud music. Watch what happens to the pepper!

Acknowledgments

I'm immensely grateful to everyone who has helped make this book possible!

An enormous thanks to Tony, my husband, for his never-ending encouragement and belief in me. From helping me test experiments, to keeping our four boys entertained and giving me time to write, you have been indispensable to getting this book to the finish line.

I couldn't have completed this book without my four sons, Nate, Dylan, Oliver and Alexander. They were my official experiment testers, and they let me know if an experiment was thumbs-up or down. They are the true heart of this book and the reason it exists, and I am eternally grateful for them.

A big note of thanks as well to my amazing publisher, Page Street Publishing, for giving me the opportunity to get this second book out into the world. Marissa Giambelluca and Meg Baskis are amazing to work with and make this process so easy with their constant support and guidance.

Thank you to Lucy Baber for the amazing photography and for really making the experiments come to life! You've been amazing to work with, especially when keeping the kids calm and entertained with fun quizzes and games when they got a bit unruly!

And last, thank you to all my Raising Dragons supporters! Nearly five years later and I'm still inspired by this community daily. You all keep me motivated and sharing my ideas with the world, and for that I'm forever thankful.

About the Author

Andrea Scalzo Yi is the founder and creative force behind Raising Dragons, a company with a mission to inspire parents and educators with simple ways to play with and educate kids. A wife and mother of four energetic sons, her background in both engineering and fashion gave her a passion for STEAM activities. This led her to create Raising Dragons (raisingdragons.com), where she shares simple, educational activities that allow parents and educators to make learning fun! Featured in articles by Hearst Digital Media, *Good Housekeeping* and Brit+Co, Raising Dragons has amassed more than 1.3 million followers across platforms including Facebook, Instagram, Pinterest and YouTube, and her videos have been viewed more than 100 million times. In 2019, she published her first book, *100 Easy STEAM Activities*, and launched her online shop RaisingDragonsShop.com, which carries a curated assortment of educational toys and kits. She resides near Philadelphia, Pennsylvania, with her family.

INDEX

A

acid-base reactions
    Dissolving Seashells, 137
    Fizzy Art, 155
    Lemon Volcano, 135
    Red Cabbage Experiment, 28–29
adhesion, 152
air density
    Diving Ketchup Packet, 123
    Dry Paper Experiment, 119
air pressure
    Blow Paper in a Bottle, 125
    Don't Open the Bottle, 126
    Lifting with Air, 122
    Rising Water Candle Experiment, 138
    Upside-Down Water Cup, 18
Aluminum Foil Boat, 136
antacid tablets, 44
anthocyanin, 28–29
arched designs
    How Strong is an Eggshell?, 50
    Standing on Eggs, 71
art projects
    Egg Art, 146
    Fizzy Art, 155
    Oil and Water Art, 145
    String Art, 142
    Sun Prints, 175
    Wet and Dry Painting, 147

B

bags
    plastic, 107
    ziplock, 50, 67, 68, 80, 128
baking soda
    DIY Fire Extinguisher, 129
    Exploding Baggie, 128
    Fizzy Art, 155
    Fluffy Slime, 98–99
    Lemon Volcano, 135
    Red Cabbage Experiment, 28–29
Balancing Can, 63
Balancing Forks, 84
Balloon Skewers, 89
balloons
    Balloon Skewers, 89
    Fill the Balloon, 120
    Floating Ring, 107
    Jumping Shapes, 90
    Pop a Balloon with a Sun Ray, 176
    Spin a Penny in a Balloon, 92
    Spinning Pencil, 93
Banana Secret Message, 59
bases. See acid-base reactions
beans, 67
Bendy Straw, 21
Bernoulli's principle, 122
black, colors of, 151
Blow Paper in a Bottle, 125
Blue Coins, 83
boat, aluminum foil, 136
bottles, 1-L plastic
    Blow Paper in a Bottle, 125
    Diving Ketchup Packet, 123
    Don't Open the Bottle, 126
bottles, 2-L plastic, 120
bottles, glass soda, 33
bottles, water
    Coin in the Bottle, 86
    Potato Skewer Balance, 111
    Spinning Forks, 60
    Spinning Pencil, 93
boxes, small, 77
bubble solution, 23
bubbles
    Smoking Bubbles, 116
    Three-Layer Bubbles, 23
    Tree-Layer Bubbles, 23
buoyancy
    Aluminum Foil Boat, 136
    Floating Orange, 43

C

cabbage leaves, 28–29
calcium carbonate
    Dissolving Seashells, 137
    Rubber Egg, 102
Can Crusher, 132
can, balancing, 63
candles
    DIY Fire Extinguisher, 129
    Rising Water Candle Experiment, 138
Candy Rainbow, 165
capillary action
    Straw Wrapper Worms, 81
    Toothpick Star, 14
carbon dioxide
    Dissolving Seashells, 137
    DIY Fire Extinguisher, 129
    Exploding Baggie, 128
    Fizzy Art, 155
    Lemon Volcano, 135
    Rubber Egg, 102
    Smoking Bubbles, 116
    Soda Volcano, 131
carrots, 111
casein molecules, 95
casein plastics, 95
center of gravity
    Balancing Can, 63
    Balancing Forks, 84
    Spinning Forks, 60
center of mass, 111
centrifugal force, 31
centripetal force
    Don't Spill the Water, 25
    Spin a Penny in a Balloon, 92
    Tornado in a Bottle, 37
checker pieces, 72
chemical bond alterations, 148
chromatography, 151
circles, 20, 173
citric acid, 135
Clean the Pennies, 97
Coffee Filter Chromatography, 151
coffee filters
    Coffee Filter Chromatography, 151
    Red Cabbage Experiment, 28
cohesion
    Magic Strainer, 33
    Water Shapes, 152
Coin in the Bottle, 86
coins
    Aluminum Foil Boat, 136
    Blue Coins, 83
    Clean the Pennies, 97
    Coin in the Bottle, 86
    Disappearing Coin, 169
    Drops on a Penny, 40
    Make a Copper-Plated Nail, 57
    Spin a Penny in a Balloon, 92
color mixing
    Candy Rainbow, 165
    Hot/Cold Watercolor Mixing, 166–167
    Playdough Color Mixing, 163
contact solution, 98–99
copper
    Blue Coins, 83
    Clean the Pennies, 97
copper citrate, 57
cornstarch, 101
cotton swab/ball
    Invisible Ink, 24
    Magic Milk, 148
Craft Stick Explosion, 104–105
crayons, 146
cream, heavy, 80
crystals, 48
cup, plastic, 177

D

density. *See also* air density
    Drinkable Density Experiment, 26
    Floating Drawings, 96
    Hot/Cold Watercolor Mixing, 166–167
diet soda, 131

difficult, simplicity level
- Can Crusher, 132
- Fluffy Slime, 98–99
- Ice Cream in a Bag, 80
- Make a Copper-Plated Nail, 57
- Red Cabbage Experiment, 28–29

Disappearing Coin, 169
dish soap
- Drops on a Penny, 40
- Floating Paper Clip, 30
- Lemon Volcano, 135
- Magic Milk, 148
- Perfect Circle, 20
- Smoking Bubbles, 116
- Swimming Fish, 39
- Tornado in a Bottle, 37

Dissolving Seashells, 137
Diving Ketchup Packet, 123
DIY Fire Extinguisher, 129
DIY Rainbow, 162
dollar bill, 122
dome, water, 34, 152
Don't Open the Bottle, 126
Don't Spill the Water, 25
Drawing a Perfect Circle, 173
Drinkable Density Experiment, 26
Drops on a Penny, 40
dry ice, 116
Dry Paper Experiment, 119
dry-erase markers, 96

E

eardrums, 177
easy, simplicity level
- Aluminum Foil Boat, 136
- Balancing Can, 63
- Balancing Forks, 84
- Balloon Skewers, 89
- Banana Secret Message, 59
- Bendy Straw, 21
- Blow Paper in a Bottle, 125
- Blue Coins, 83
- Candy Rainbow, 165
- Clean the Pennies, 97
- Coffee Filter Chromatography, 151
- Coin in the Bottle, 86
- Disappearing Coin, 169
- Dissolving Seashells, 137
- Diving Ketchup Packet, 123
- DIY Rainbow, 162
- Don't Spill the Water, 25
- Drawing a Perfect Circle, 173
- Drinkable Density Experiment, 26
- Drops on a Penny, 40
- Dry Paper Experiment, 119
- Egg Art, 146
- Egg Drop, 108

Exploding Baggie, 128
Fill the Balloon, 120
Fireworks in a Jar, 156
Fizzy Art, 155
Floating Drawings, 96
Floating Orange, 43
Floating Paper Clip, 30
Floating Ping Pong Ball, 34
Hot/Cold Watercolor Mixing, 166–167
How Strong is an Eggshell?, 50
Ice Tunnels, 78
Inertia Checkers, 72
Invisible Ink, 24
Jumping Shapes, 90
Lifting with Air, 122
Magic Milk, 148
Magic Strainer, 33
Make a Sunset, 161
Melting Ice with Pressure, 113
Notepad Friction, 87
Ocean in a Jar, 44
Oil and Ice Density, 38
Oil and Water Art, 145
One-Sided Paper: Möbius Strip, 54
Oobleck, 101
Pencils Through a Baggie, 68

Perfect Circle, 20
Playdough Color Mixing, 163
Pop a Balloon with a Sun Ray, 176
Reverse the Image, 170
Ringing Spoon, 174
Rising Water Candle Experiment, 138
Rubber Egg, 102
Separating Salt and Pepper, 73
Smoking Bubbles, 116
Sound You Can See, 177
Spin a Penny in a Balloon, 92
Spin the Bowl, 31
Spinning Eggs, 56
Spinning Forks, 60
Spinning Pencil, 93
Sprouts in a Bag, 67
Standing on Eggs, 71
Straw in a Potato, 53
Straw Wrapper Worms, 81
Sun Prints, 175
Tear the Paper, 51
Three-Layer Bubbles, 23
Toothpick Star, 14
Tornado in a Bottle, 37
Turn Milk into Plastic, 95
Underwater Volcano, 17

Upside-Down Spoon Experiment, 168
Upside-Down Water Cup, 18
Water Rainbow, 172
Water Shapes, 152
Wet and Dry Painting, 147
Whip Off the Napkin, 112
Egg Art, 146
Egg Drop, 108
eggs
    Egg Art, 146
    Egg Drop, 108
    How Strong is an Eggshell?, 50
    Rubber Egg, 102
    Spinning Eggs, 56
    Standing on Eggs, 71
elasticity, 89
energy
    Craft Stick Explosion, 104–105
    Melting Ice with Pressure, 113
Epsom salt, 48
Exploding Baggie, 128

F

fat molecules, 148
Fill the Balloon, 120
fire extinguisher, 129
Fireworks in a Jar, 156
fish, swimming, 39

Fizzy Art, 155
flashlight, 161
flight, 122
Floating Drawings, 96
Floating Heart, 74
Floating Orange, 43
Floating Paper Clip, 30
Floating Ping Pong Ball, 34
Floating Ring, 107
flow resistance, 101
Fluffy Slime, 98–99
food coloring
    Egg Art, 146
    Fireworks in a Jar, 156
    Fizzy Art, 155
    Fluffy Slime, 98–99
    Growing Crystals, 48
    Hot/Cold Watercolor Mixing, 166–167
    Ice Tunnels, 78
    Lemon Volcano, 135
    Magic Milk, 148
    Mixing Colors, 159
    Ocean in a Jar, 44
    Oil and Water Art, 145
    Oobleck, 101
    Pencils Through a Baggie, 68
    Rising Water Candle Experiment, 138
    Rubber Egg, 102
    String Art, 142

Turn Milk into Plastic, 95
Underwater Volcano, 17
Water Shapes, 152
Wet and Dry Painting, 147
force. *See also* gravity; inertia
    Don't Spill the Water, 25
    Floating Hearts, 74
    Magic Strainer, 33
    Spin a Penny in a Balloon, 92
    Spin the Bowl, 31
    Standing on Eggs, 71
    Tornado in a Bottle, 37
    Upside-Down Water Cup, 18
forks
    Balancing Forks, 84
    Spinning Forks, 60
freezing points
    Ice Cream in a Bag, 80
    Ice Tunnels, 78
friction
    Notepad Friction, 87
    Spin the Bowl, 31
fruit baskets, 77

G

germination, 67
glue, 98–99
grapes, 111
gravity. *See also* center of gravity
    Aluminum Foil Boat, 136
    Coin in the Bottle, 86
    Don't Spill the Water, 25
    Egg Drop, 108
    Wall Marble Run, 77
Growing Crystals, 48

H

hair dryer, 122
heat transfer
    Can Crusher, 132
    Fill the Balloon, 120
    Fireworks in a Jar, 156
    Hot/Cold Watercolor Mixing, 166–167
    Ice Cream in a Bag, 80
    Rising Water Candle Experiment, 138
    Toothpick Star, 14
    Underwater Volcano, 17
Hot/Cold Watercolor Mixing, 166–167
How Strong is an Eggshell?, 50
hydrochloric acid, 97
hydronium ions, 28–29
hydroxide ions, 28–29

I

ice
    Can Crusher, 132
    Fill the Balloon, 120
    Hot/Cold Watercolor Mixing, 166–167
    Ice Tunnels, 78
    Melting Ice with Pressure, 113
    Oil and Ice Density, 38
    Smoking Bubbles, 116
Ice Cream in a Bag, 80
Ice Tunnels, 78
inertia
    Coin in the Bottle, 86
    Egg Drop, 108
    Inertia Checkers, 72
    Spinning Eggs, 56
    Straw in a Potato, 53
    Whip Off the Napkin, 112
Inertia Checkers, 72
Invisible Ink, 24
ions, 28–29

J

juices, 26, 28. *See also* lemons/lemon juice
Jumping Shapes, 90

K

ketchup packet, 123
kinetic energy, 104–105

L

lava lamps, 44
lava, volcano, 17
Lemon Volcano, 135
lemons/lemon juice
    Invisible Ink, 24
    Lemon Volcano, 135

Make a Copper-Plated Nail, 57
Ocean in a Jar, 44
Red Cabbage Experiment, 28–29
levitation, 107
Lifting with Air, 122
light rays
　Disappearing Coin, 169
　Pop a Balloon with a Sun Ray, 176
　Sun Prints, 175
　Upside-Down Spoon Experiment, 168
　Water Rainbow, 172
light waves
　DIY Rainbow, 162
　Make a Sunset, 161
　Sun Prints, 175
light, bending of, 21
limes, 44

M

M&Ms, 165
Magic Milk, 148
Magic Strainer, 33
Magic Twirling Paper, 64
magnesium sulfate, 48
magnetism, 74
magnifying glasses, 176
Make a Copper-Plated Nail, 57
Make a Sunset, 161
marbles, 77

markers
　Coffee Filter Chromatography, 151
　Don't Open the Bottle, 126
　Floating Drawings, 96
　Reverse the Image, 170
medium, simplicity level
　Craft Stick Explosion, 104–105
　DIY Fire Extinguisher, 129
　Don't Open the Bottle, 126
　Floating Heart, 74
　Floating Ring, 107
　Growing Crystals, 48
　Lemon Volcano, 135
　Magic Twirling Paper, 64
　Potato Skewer Balance, 111
　Soda Volcano, 131
　String Art, 142
　Swimming Fish, 39
　Wall Marble Run, 77
Melting Ice with Pressure, 113
Mentos mints, 131
mesh, 33
messages, secret. See secret messages
metals, washing, 97
milk
　Magic Milk, 148
　Make a Sunset, 161
　Turn Milk into Plastic, 95
mints, Mentos, 131

mirrors
　DIY Rainbow, 162
　Upside-Down Spoon Experiment, 168
Mixing Colors, 159
Möbius strips, 54
molecule expansion
　Floating Paper Clip, 30
　Underwater Volcano, 17
motion, first law of. See inertia

N

nails, 57
napkins, 112
newspaper, 77
Newton's first law of motion. See inertia
non-Newtonian fluids, 98–99, 101
notecards, 166–167
Notepad Friction, 87

O

Ocean in a Jar, 44
Oil and Ice Density, 38
Oil and Water Art, 145
oil and water reactions. See polar vs nonpolar molecules
One-Sided Paper: Möbius Strip, 54
Oobleck, 101

oxidization
    Banana Secret Message, 59
    Invisible Ink, 24

P

paint, sidewalk, 101
paper
    Blow Paper in a Bottle, 125
    Coin in the Bottle, 86
    Drawing a Perfect Circle, 173
    Dry Paper Experiment, 119
    Hot/Cold Watercolor Mixing, 166–167
    Invisible Ink, 24
    Lifting with Air, 122
    Notepad Friction, 87
    One-Sided Paper: Möbius Strip, 54
    Reverse the Image, 170
    Soda Volcano, 131
    String Art, 142
    Sun Prints, 175
    Swimming Fish, 39
    Tear the Paper, 51
    Upside-Down Water Cup, 18
    Water Rainbow, 172
paper clips
    Floating Heart, 74
    Floating Paper Clip, 30
paper rolls, empty (toilet or paper towel)
    Egg Drop, 108
    Wall Marble Run, 77
paper tearing, 51
patina, 83
pecans, 44
pencils
    Drawing a Perfect Circle, 173
    Pencils through a Baggie, 68
    Spinning Pencil, 93
Pencils Through a Baggie, 68
pennies. *See also* coins
    Clean the Pennies, 97
    Drops on a Penny, 40
    Make a Copper-Plated Nail, 57
    Spin a Penny in a Balloon, 92
pepper
    Separating Salt and Pepper, 73
    Sound You Can See, 177
Perfect Circle, 20
pH indicators, 28–29
pin, 126
ping pong balls
    Floating Ping Pong Ball, 34
    Lifting with Air, 122
plants, 14, 67, 81, 147
plastic spoons, 73
plastic wrap, 177
plastics, casein, 95
playdough
    Magic Twirling Paper, 64
    Playdough Color Mixing, 163
Playdough Color Mixing, 163
polar vs nonpolar molecules
    Egg Art, 146
    Fireworks in a Jar, 156
    Ocean in a Jar, 44
    Oil and Ice Density, 38
    Oil and Water Art, 145
polymers
    Balloon Skewers, 89
    Fluffy Slime, 98–99
    Pencils Through a Baggie, 68
polyphenol oxidase, 59
Pop a Balloon with a Sun Ray, 176
Potato Skewer Balance, 111
potatoes
    Potato Skewer Balance, 111
    Straw in a Potato, 53
potential energy, 104–105
pressure
    How Strong is an Eggshell?, 50
    Melting Ice with Pressure, 113
    Oobleck, 101
    Upside-Down Water Cup, 18
primary/secondary colors. *See* color mixing

R

rainbows
- Candy Rainbow, 165
- DIY Rainbow, 162
- Playdough Color Mixing, 163
- Water Rainbow, 172

Red Cabbage Experiment, 28–29
reflection, 168
refraction
- Bendy Straw, 21
- Disappearing Coin, 168
- Reverse the Image, 170

release agents, 96
Reverse the Image, 170
Ringing Spoon, 174
Rising Water Candle Experiment, 138
rubber bands, 177
Rubber Egg, 102

S

salt
- Clean the Pennies, 97
- crystals, 48
- Ice Cream in a Bag, 80
- Ice Tunnels, 78
- Separating Salt and Pepper, 73

seashells, 137
secondary colors. *See* color mixing

secret messages
- Banana Secret Message, 59
- Egg Art, 146
- Invisible Ink, 24

seeds, 67
Separating Salt and Pepper, 73
shaving cream, 98–99
sidewalk paint, 101
silicone oils, 96
simplicity levels. *See* difficult, simplicity level; easy, simplicity level; medium, simplicity level

skewers, wooden
- Balloon Skewers, 89
- Potato Skewer Balance, 111

Skittles, 165
slime, 98–99
Smoking Bubbles, 116
soda cans
- Balancing Can, 63
- Can Crusher, 132

Soda Volcano, 131
sodium citrate, 135
sound waves
- Ringing Spoon, 174
- Sound You Can See, 177

Sound You Can See, 177
Spin a Penny in a Balloon, 92
Spin the Bowl, 31
Spinning Eggs, 56
Spinning Forks, 60
Spinning Pencil, 93

spoons
- Ringing Spoon, 174
- Upside-Down Spoon Experiment, 168

Sprouts in a Bag, 67
Standing on Eggs, 71
static electricity
- Floating Ring, 107
- Jumping Shapes, 90
- Separating Salt and Pepper, 73
- Spinning Pencil, 93

Straw in a Potato, 53
Straw Wrapper Worms, 81
straw wrappers, 81
straws
- Bendy Straw, 21
- Blow Paper in a Bottle, 125
- Straw in a Potato, 53
- Three-Layer Bubbles, 23

string
- Ringing Spoon, 174
- String Art, 142

String Art, 142
sugar
- Drinkable Density Experiment, 26
- Ice Cream in a Bag, 80
- Red Cabbage Experiment, 28–29

Sun Prints, 175
sunlight
    DIY Rainbow, 162
    Make a Sunset, 161
    Pop a Balloon with a Sun Ray, 176
    Sun Prints, 175
    Water Rainbow, 172
supersaturated solutions, 48
surface tension
    Don't Open the Bottle, 126
    Drops on a Penny, 40
    Floating Paper Clip, 30
    Floating Ping Pong Ball, 34
    Magic Milk, 148
    Magic Strainer, 33
    Perfect Circle, 20
    Swimming Fish, 39
    Three-Layer Bubbles, 23
    Water Shapes, 152
surfaces, 54
Swimming Fish, 39
symmetry, 142

T

tattoos, temporary, 96
Tear the Paper, 51
thread
    Floating Heart, 74
    Perfect Circle, 20
    String Art, 142

Three-Layer Bubbles, 23
tissue paper
    Floating Heart, 74
    Jumping Shapes, 90
    Magic Twirling Paper, 64
Toothpick Star, 14
toothpicks
    Balancing Forks, 84
    Banana Secret Message, 59
    Magic Strainer, 33
    Toothpick Star, 14
Tornado in a Bottle, 37
Turn Milk into Plastic, 95

U

ultraviolet light, 175
Underwater Volcano, 17
Upside-Down Spoon Experiment, 168
Upside-Down Water Cup, 18

V

vanilla extract, 80
vegetable oil
    Fireworks in a Jar, 156
    Ocean in a Jar, 44
    Oil and Ice Density, 38
    Oil and Water Art, 145
verdigris, 83
vinegar
    Blue Coins, 83
    Clean the Pennies, 97

Dissolving Seashells, 137
DIY Fire Extinguisher, 129
Egg Art, 146
Exploding Baggie, 128
Fizzy Art, 155
Make a Copper-Plated Nail, 57
Red Cabbage Experiment, 28–29
Rubber Egg, 102
Tornado in a Bottle, 37
Turn Milk into Plastic, 95
viscosity, 101
volcanoes
    Lemon Volcano, 135
    Soda Volcano, 131
    Underwater Volcano, 17
vortices, 37

W

Wall Marble Run, 77
water bottles. *See* bottles, water
Water Rainbow, 172
Water Shapes, 152
Wet and Dry Painting, 147
Whip Off the Napkin, 112
white light. *See* sunlight

Z

Ziplock bags. *See under* bags